Karma

MY JOURNEY

Karma Sammy

Copyright © 2014 by Karma Sammy

KARMA
My Journey
By Karma Sammy

Printed in the United States of America
Edited by Xulon Press

ISBN 9781498413916

All rights reserved solely by the author. The author guarantees all contents are original and do not infringe upon the legal rights of any other person or work. No part of this book may be reproduced in any form without the permission of the author. The views expressed in this book are not necessarily those of the publisher.

Scripture quotations taken fromthe King James Version (KJV) – *public domain*.

www.xulonpress.com

TABLE OF CONTENTS

Introduction: Trinidad – A Tropical Paradise xiii

Chapter 1: My Journey Begins 19
Chapter 2: A Living Hell. 33
Chapter 3: But God 50
Chapter 4; All Things New. 63
Chapter 5: God Makes a Way 81
Chapter 6: From Tragedy to Triumph 96
Chapter 7: Nothing Is Impossible for Our God 109
Chapter 8: A Year of Changes and Miracles 130
Chapter 9: Blessed Are They that Mourn for They
           Shall be comforted. 147

Conclusion. 165

ACKNOWLEDGEMENTS!!

This book is dedicated in the loving memory of my beloved parents, for their love and determination and the many sacrifices to go the extra miles with hopes and faith in God to save my life,

To my Siblings!!

To my siblings who suffered along with my parents their braveness and courage as they live each day in fear and remain strong and their faith in God for me that I would live, I m ever grateful to them! I love you all very much. God richly bless you all.

My Husband!!

To my loving husband and Children for your love pray and support thank you all so much you mean everything to me and most of all my Grand kids whom I love and cherish you are my pride and joy, I praise God for each of you may the love of the lord overflows within us as we walk in the lord.

My sincere gratitude to the churches that stood with my parents and for their constant prayer and encouragement and the Pastors who was obedient to the lord and took time to minister to them and gave them hope in the lord may God bless him.

Many thanks to my dearest friend Michelle for your love and generous support for your constant prayer you are the best Thank you for being my friend love always.

Glory to God!

To God be the Glory and honor and praise for Jesus Christ the Savior of my life, whom to know is life eternal and in him I live and move and have my being. In all I do I stand in awe of him. For all the blessings He bestow upon my life I continue to live in Him, I'm the righteous of God in Christ Jesus our Lord.

Profile on Karma:

Karma a very powerful Woman of God a pray warrior an inspiration to many very dedicated to God and the calling in her life she speaks with boldness and much authority in the lord. She's heartwarming and hospitable a blessings to everyone she meets an amazing and virtuous woman never afraid of a challenge stands strong in her faith in God she always wear an inviting smile, and truly radiates the love of God.

Residence! Karma resides in Portland Oregon with her husband who's a minister of the Gospel and is a freelance Preacher together they had five kids two went to be with the lord. Their two daughters and their husband live in Oregon with their kids they are currently serving the lord and following the call in their lives. Their only son resides in Trinidad they have seven grand children's whom they love and adore very much their gifts from God.

Special thanks to the team at Xulon Press.

FORWORD:

My Journey

I'm borrowing the words of Pope John Paul II that he used to describe the movie "The Passion of the Christ" to label what I have known of Karma Sammy and what I have read in her book. He said "It is as it was".

This short essay is simple, but sublime. Its message is personal yet all compassing. It is for anyone yet has an appeal for everyone regardless of age, greed, color, race, nationally or spiritual maturity.

If you follow her steps in this book you'll discover that her steps will follow you. It will identify with you in your past and current stations in life and beyond that it will nudge you on the way forward.

This compact book is Christ revealing, God glorifying, and self-edifying.

Sincerely

Anthony K Kawalsingh (B.Th, M.Th, Lit.D) Senior Pastor

PREFACE:

In the past 25 plus years of ministry my wife, Lori, and I have met many wonderful and amazing people, Karma Sammy and her husband Ken are two such people. We first met their adult children as they came into our lives and our church family here in Portland, Oregon several years ago. As we watched God's transforming power do a great work in their children and grandchildren, we then met Ken and Karma, whom we realized were a key to the family's transformation. As the old saying goes "never underestimate the power of a praying mom or grandmother".

Over the past few years we have gotten to know the Sammy's and they are a precious and valuable part of our church and lives. Knowing the back story as I now do, knowing what they have been through, seeing that they never gave up on God or blame Him for their struggles, watching them love everyone who crosses their path… makes me love them even more. They are tireless, faithful servants of our Lord and Savior, Jesus Christ. They are people that use the sum of all they have experienced to reach out and help others.

Jesus taught in Matthew chapter 7 that if a person listens to His teachings and obeys them that he or she will be like a person that built their house on a solid foundation. When the storms come, the house will stand. The storms of life have come to the Sammy's and yet their lives still stand as a testimony to the Lord because they built their house on the Rock of Jesus Christ.

As you read the amazing story of God's deliverance and redemption of a little girl's life in Trinidad, I pray that you are able to grow in the knowledge of His Son, Jesus Christ and His power to set man free from sin, bondage and sorrow. It is my prayer that you will see that Jesus is the only true answer to new life. Let this story of one woman's faith in God in the face of test and trial move you closer to Him.

In His Love and Service,
JD Henderson
Pastor, Life Christian Center
Portland, Oregon
September, 2014

INTRODUCTION

Trinidad–A Tropical Paradise

I was born on the beautiful island of Trinidad and Tobago located in the Caribbean off the coast of South America. Sometimes known as the West Indies, Trinidad is known as the land of steel pan and calypso music. And the land of hummingbirds, also the scarlet ibis, which is the national bird, and is featured on the coat of arms of Trinidad Tobago. People travel from around the world to watch the many beautiful species of birds that nest on our island. It's a breathtaking place to visit. The beaches are beautiful line with coconut palm trees white sand blue water. It's just marvelous making it a wonderful tropical paradise. The beauty and wonder of this country is amazing.

The island is also known for its colorful culture and wide variety of delicious foods. To name a few delicacies I grew up to love and enjoy. A typical menu dish is stewed chicken, white rice, red beans, fried plantains, and homemade ginger beer. Curried chicken, potatoes, *channa* known as garbanzos beans and *roti, which is a type of flat, bread* a traditional favorites. Roti is sold in many Indian restaurants in Trinidad; it's served with meat of your choice chicken roti, beef roti, potato roti or vegetable roti. **Dhal Puri** a roti filled with spiced, cooked, split pea filling. Dhal Puri is considered to be a celebratory roti as it is generally made on weekends, on holidays and at festivals. Served in most homes.

Another roti is Paratha which is layered pastry. A different type of flat bread this type of roti is usually served with sautéed vegetables curry meat of choice or fish and a choka. A fire-roasted vegetable ground or pureed and seasoned with garlic, chilies, tamarind or green mango.

Fried bake deep fried bread made from unleavened dough usually served with: salted fish. Corned beef, or smoke herring, served with fresh peppers, tomatoes, onions cucumbers and sometime bacon, fried plantain, stewed chicken, Coconut bake is usually served with fried Accra salt-fish fritters. Another very popular and nationally well-known dish is callaloo, which is a creamy, spicy dish made of dasheen leaves, know as Taro leaves, okra locally known as Okro, crab or pigtails, thyme, coconut milk, Callaloo is often served with cornmeal coo-coo, plantain, sweet potatoes, dumplings, curried crab, or Marconi pie, and fried rice.

Avery popular dish is Pelau cook with pigeon peas chicken, or beef, carrots fresh herbs with coconut milk. The entire dish is flavored and colored with caramelized brown Sugar. This Pelau is a one-pot dish and is served with a spicy salad of choice. Is made on weekends and especially when family and friends get together for a lime Caribbean word for get-together.

An array of fish can be bought at local markets throughout Trinidad and Tobago, such as red fish, lobsters salmon flying

Introduction

fish, conch, crab tilapia. To name a few the citizens, accompanies their meals with various condiments which can include pepper sauces, chutneys, and pickles are often homemade.

There are many different popular beverages in Trinidad. These include, various sweet drinks Sodas Peardrax Malta, Smalta, Shandy, ginger beer, Guinness Beer, sorrel, mauby, seamoss punch, soursop punch, Coca Cola, and Coconut water can be found. Throughout the Island serving local favorites, home-made wines, and many others from local fruits.

Visitors from all over the world come to experience the culture and the great hospitality of the citizens. There's a lot to enjoy in Trinidad and Tobago.

Culture

The citizens of Trinidad hold strongly to their many religious beliefs and cultures. Muslim festival is celebrated, with a time of fasting and end with a feast of foods and sweets. Shared with relatives and friends Indian weddings are also known for their drums beating music. When the drums are heard in the villages it serves as a time to celebrate with songs and dance an invitation to happiness. Food is served to all who join the celebration. Food is important in all religious occasscions.

The twin island states is unique in the fact it's the home of many different religions beliefs too many to mention. Most common are Roman Catholics. And Anglicans, The largest of the religious groups are the Christians; this group is the fastest growing group, with Evangelicals, Pentecostals and Charismatic. Spiritual Baptist, Hindus and Muslims makes up the next three large groups. Several other smaller groups are among those that makes Trinidad and Tobago a multi-religious country.

The islands of Trinidad and Tobago are famous for its steel band pan music. This music is an important part of Carnival, the biggest celebration of the year. Carnival is a giant celebration that happens before Lent every year. There are many parties and parades where thousands of people dress up in the most flamboyant costumes and dance to calypso and steel pan music. This is very colorful and full of fun for everyone. Calypso music and the steel pan which is widely claimed to be the only acoustic musical instrument invented during the 20th century. The diverse cultural and religious background allow for many festivities and ceremonies throughout the year. Soca is a dance music which is a mix of Trinidad's calypso and East Indian music and rhythms, especially chutney music. It combines the melodic sound of calypso. Bands often form in the major cities of Trinidad and Tobago. Band members dress in costumes and dance in large groups on the streets of the cities.

Carnival, the most influential, single cultural factor in Trinidad and Tobago. Originally a day time celebration where people rode the streets in floats, or watched from the upper stories of residences and businesses. The first few hours of Carnival were Monday morning from about 4 am until sunrise and were known as *J'ouvert* this allowed the wealthy to mix with the poor.

The daytime celebration of Carnival on Monday and Tuesday is dominated by costumed masqueraders. The Carnival season begins on Boxing Day December 26 and soca and calypso music reign supreme over the airwaves.

Introduction

The festivity takes place from year end through. February or at the beginning of lent are generally. Theme and feature live music from bands and. soca artists who are promoting their song contributions for the year. Trinidad carnival is the largest tourist's attraction. visitors pour in each year to enjoy this fantastic event.

At Christmas time, *parang* is the traditional form of music. *Pastelle* black fruit cake, sweet bread is customary foods, and *ponche de crème eggnog*, ginger beer, and sorrel local homemade wines are the drinks. Most families enjoy making these treats Christmas another big celebrations. Is widely celebrated by everyone no matter color creed race or religion everyone has an equal place. Divali is a Hindu festival, a celebration of the victory of good over evil. Trinidad and Tobago. A nation with many celebrations, the citizens love to party they know how to enjoy life. Visitors travel from all over the world to take part in these celebrations and have a fabulous time.

This is a very blessed island. I was privileged to be born here in the days when sugarcane was a big industry. Trinidad and Tobago exports bauxite petroleum sugar, oil cocoa, coffee, coconut, and a variety of citrus fruits. The people grow most of their own foods and share with their relatives, neighbors, and friends. When there is a surplus, they sell at roadside markets. Trinidad has been the largest oil and gas producing industries in the Caribbean. And also generates ammonia and several methanol plants. Truly this nations is a bless paradise. Our Motto: Together we aspire together we achieve.

Chapter 1
MY JOURNEY BEGINS

On May 2, 1955, my mother gave birth to her second child, a baby girl at Mabel Daniel's house, better known as Aunty May. My parents were so happy. They already had one child a son. My parents, Seepersad Nangoo and Sylvia Roster, met at the Hilton hotel where my father worked as a handyman and my mother worked as a housekeeper. They fell in love and decided to live together outside of marriage as my dad had already been married when he met my mom. In those days there was no marriage register to sign in the Hindu Religion. The Hindu Priest did the marriage ceremony that was considered legal by their relatives. My father left his former wife and married my mother after their fourth baby, my sister, was born. They had more kids after they were married. I have six brothers and one sister. My parents were married together for thirty-five years until my father passed away at the age of seventy-five. My mother remained a widow and lived among her children.

My Mother traveled to the United States where she lived with me for nine months, but she missed the life she was accustomed to with all her other children. She decided she did not like life in the US and went back to Trinidad where she lived the rest of her life amongst her children and grandchildren. She passed away at the age of sixty-four. Sadly, I was not there at the time of her passing.

I missed her last days and could not be at her side. As I was in very poor health myself recovering from a serious heart condition. I wanted so much to be there with her just to see her one last time. I loved her so much and it broke my heart. I was unable to be at her side and hold the hands that held mine as. I grew up under her care. Those hands had carried me through many of my life's ups and downs. Her hands wiped my tears, I still think of her blessed hands that gave me her special touch. All she had to endure and sacrifice for her children. She was always there when I needed her; I could not be there when she passed from this life. Upon my doctor's advice, I was not physically able to make the all day flight to Trinidad to attend her funeral. This grieved me terribly. I miss her and carry the memories of my mom in my heart still today. She was a very precious woman to me.

A few years later I was able to visit Trinidad and spend time with my brothers. I went to my mom's house and felt as if she was still there. I never had the chance to say a physical good-bye to her, just being in her house helped me move on with my life, as I dealt with the pain of her death. I thought about all the ways my mom was special to me, I especially admired her inner strength and the courage she showed me growing up. My father was very abusive to her mentally and physically. As a young child that was horrible to me. My Mom had no way of getting us out of that life so she showed us how to live through it. One thing we all knew, we did not want to live that way when we grew up. Life was unsure and very hard for us kids, but somehow we all made it through.

My Near Death Experience

At one point, my mother was not sure I would make it through my first year of life. As a four-month-old baby, I became very sick and close to death. During those times doctors had very little medical knowledge, and not much medical advice was given to the sick. My Parents did what they could with the hope I would get well and live. The doctor told my parents. I had contracted a deadly fever. He was not sure if it was Scarlet Fever or some kind of Rheumatic Fever, he said to them anyone who contracted Scarlet Fever rarely, if ever survived. The doctor gave them different kinds of medicines to give me to try to make me better. They tried everything and worried what would happen if the medicine did not work for me.

My father turned to his Hindu priest for magic formulas and asked the priest to use his Hindu practices to seek a healing for me, as my condition worsened. My mother was a Catholic when she met my father she converted to Hinduism to marry him. As my condition worsened, she turned back to her Catholic belief to see if this would help. Needless to say neither of their "religions" worked, and it appeared I was going to die. They never gave me a name for fear I would not live as my parents did not want a curse to fall on them.

Desperate, my mom went to visit her father and told him all what was happening to me and what the doctor had told them. My grandfather believed in witchcraft and black magic. Believing that my death was imminent, he told my parents he knew what to do so I would live. He had my parents bring me to him and stay with him and complied with his request. His practice was very mystical; they believed in what he does will work. He asked them to gather up nine different bean seeds and herbs and placed them in a bowl for him. Then for the next nine days, at a certain time every day, my mom took me to him and he would give me a spiritual bath with the beans and herbs. After the baths, is finish he specified the stuff had to be planted in the ground and the produce was not to be reaped for eating? It should remain on the vines until it dried up, fell to the ground, and died. The plants were not to be cut down. They were to remain and allowed to dry and wither away. My desperate parents did as my grandfather requested them and every day I showed signs of life. They could not understand it; all they knew is I lived.

A "Chosen Name"

When I safely reached the age of one, my parents decided it was safe to give me a name. Up until that point my parents called me daughter because the Hindus believe in reincarnation. If they had a sick child and expected that child to die, they would not name the child. Their thinking was they never knew who or what that child would reincarnate to be in the next life. This was their belief if a baby died with a name that brought a curse, a bad sign, bad luck or bad omen on the family.

They went to the Hindu priest who was my father's spiritual counselor and had performed their marriage ceremony. It took the priest five days of religious ceremonial offerings to the Hindu gods before he could find the right name for me. Then he gave me the mystic name, Karma. This was a very "chosen name" for me and indicated to my parents how I should live, and the things I had to be taught to do as I grew up in the Hindu religion. This name made me the chosen one in the family. I never did understand why me since I had an older brother, yet it had to be me. From then on the traditions and teachings of the Hindu life were given to me.

As I began to grow up under my father's Hindu beliefs, we had many ceremonial duties to perform every morning. We had to give a spiritual pitcher of water to the sunrise for the blessing of that day. Every evening I had to light a spiritual light to the going down of the sun right at sunset. I had to have daily spiritual baths and say spiritual chants as a prayer to all the different gods. As a child, this was not fun and I hated it. I never had any understanding of what I was doing or saying to the gods every day. We did the same chants this was not spoken in English so it was hard for us to understand. The prayers were spoken in Hindi one of the East Indian languages. There were many gods to worship. As children, we had to obey and do what we were told. Sometimes we would have days of fasting and worship at our house where the whole family and visits from relatives and neighbors would come to celebrate with us. These were ceremonial sacrifices to the gods performed by the priest with lots of flowers and foods. To receive some kind of blessings, of good fortune this was a religious way of life for many of the people all around us as well.

My Paternal Grandfather

I remember my paternal grandfather had a special love for me. We lived across the street from him and every day he would come and take me home with him. Everywhere he went he took me with him. He called me his Karri. Some of my cousins still call me that name today. I knew I was special to him even though he had many granddaughters. I remember walking to the neighbors in the village with him. He always said I was his little Karri.

One day I was with him, when he suddenly collapsed. I did not know what happened. I thought he must have gotten sick. A week later my dad told me he had gone away. I didn't know he had died; I thought he had gone to visit a relative far away. I knew he had lots of relatives. Living far in other villages, I missed him coming for me every day. This was hard for me to understand as a little girl. Why he was gone so long. Then my dad told me he was never coming back. This was a sad time for the entire family. As I grew older I learn about death then I knew. I will never see him again. I miss him more and more everyday as I grew up. soon things in our home deteriorated after his sudden death.

Living Under Verbal and Physical Abuse

We lived from day to day as my father became an alcoholic and a womanizer. We were all very afraid of him. The physical and verbal abuse was terrible and steadily worsened.

My Journey Begins

My mother was abused almost every day which made us kids begin to hate our father. He never showed us any sort of love. We were never treated as his children; instead we were like little slaves. We had daily chores to do. There's no running water in the house. We lived in the country and only one water tap available in the village. All the villagers would go to fetch their daily water supply from this tap. We had to get up very early in the morning to fetch clean water.

My father made us a little make shift box cart with little wheels to roll and a piece of rope for a handle to steer. So we did not run off the road. We would place six water gallons on the cart and off we'd go down the street headed for the water tap. We had to go downhill and uphill which was very hard for us as young children. We'd do this again and again until the water barrels were full. Afterwards we had to feed the ducks, chickens, and pigs before my father wakeup, and before getting ready for school. After a quick breakfast, we'd walk five miles to school, by the time we got to school we were too tired to learn much.

However, school days became an escape for us. We were free from the drama of an abusive home for which we were grateful. We were free to laugh and play like children even only for a short time. We knew when we got back home; the chores would start all over again. This never ended for us kids. We were never allowed any playtime with our cousins or the neighbor kids. We never had much free time to enjoy kids stuff. We were always busy, my father made sure of that. He was very protective and kept us going all the time. Life was very hard especially when he was drunk and abusive. He would embarrass us and beat us if we did not do as he said. We were always so scared of him. We learned early on what to expect from him we tried to do what was right at all times.

We attended a Catholic school since this was the only school in the village even though we were raised believing in the Hindu faith. School was a privilege for me as a small child. I could only attend two days one week and then three days the next week depending on where my parents had to work. I was not allowed to run and play with other kids at school like my siblings. Because I missed so many lessons, I was always behind in my classes. I had to remain in the classroom to catch up with my lessons while everyone else was allowed to go outside and play. I tried hard, but my learning ability was very poor making it very difficult for me to catch up with my classmates. I loved reading, spelling, English, and penmanship. I never liked math. I would be at the bottom of the class in every subject which was very embarrassing to me. I always got picked on because I could not keep up. I tried, but I missed too many days of teaching in every subject. I was never happy with my schoolwork my siblings did so much better than I did growing up.

As we grew older and completed primary school, we were told by our parents they could not afford to send us to high school. We finished school with an eighth grade education. My sister was the only one fortunate enough to attend a Christian high school; she never graduated as money was always an issue. None of us were able to earn any degree of any kind. In place of high school, I was sent to learn to sew and make

My Journey Begins

women's clothing. I loved sewing and was glad this was the choice they made for me.

We lived in a small village in the country surrounded by sugar cane plantations. Most of the neighbors worked in the cane fields to earn a living. Cutting sugar cane was very hard work. My parents worked in the sugarcane fields and rice fields. My father was also a fish vendor in the village. He worked hard to earn money, but never really cared about our needs for school supplies and textbooks. We always had to borrow from our cousins for our needs while he used his money to satisfy his greedy life style of drinking and womanizing. My mother stayed in this marriage and endured the abuse day after day. If she leaves he would bring her back. This was tough for me being the oldest girl; I had to take care of my younger siblings. She was a strong woman, she exhibited a lot of courage she had a kind heart. She always made sure we had food every day no matter how little it was or how abusive my father has been to her.

We never had much to wear; my father never gave her money to take care of the household needs. When he was not drunk, he did the shopping, but never cared about important things. Mother always managed to get us through somehow. Even though she was very afraid of him, she did what she needed to do to survive. She knew what to expect when he came home after a drunken binge, as hard as this was for her, she had courage to live for her children. She was very strong a hard worker. She remained faithful in the marriage even though it was hard for her and for her children good mother, the best! I loved her dearly! A woman of great courage!

Tolerance and patience to live with my father during those abusive years. She was a survivor!

It Was a Living Hell

We lived across the street from my father's two brothers and his mother. There was hardly a time when there was not some kind of conflict or family feud going on between them. They never got along so we never could get along with our cousins either. We all attended the Catholic school in the area and would sometimes get into big fights with them. We'd go home to complain to our parents and then the feud would ignite again. My father had a very hostile way of handling any kind of conflict. He was a very angry, violent man. Even his brothers were afraid of him. Always ready to settle any conflict in a man to man fist fight or he would threaten to kill them. No one ever dared challenge him and the conflicts never came to an end. This continued all through our childhood.

We were surrounded by a lot of family confusion, violence, and physical and verbal abuse. There was no escape for us kids. He had no mercy if we did not do as we were told or refused to complete a chore; he would beat us to the point where we could no longer cry. Sometimes. Not able to breathe. We received cuts and bruises from all the beatings. He was so cruel he sends us to the bathroom before the beatings start so we did not wet our pants. We were scared to death of him. No one would dare come to rescue us, not even our own mother or she would get a beating also.

Our father would go out to have a good time every Friday night, and come home drunk and start cursing at our mother.

Almost as soon as he got in the house he would start beating her for absolutely nothing. We start screaming so people could come to rescue her, no one ever came. My older brother and I would jump through the window and run as fast as we could to his brothers' house across the street. Even though we knew they were afraid of him, this was our only chance to save our mother from his rage. We did this over and over again until one night we got caught and got a beating we would never forget.

It was a living hell! My growing up years was horrible! We lived in constant fear of our lives and for the life of our mother. My siblings and I grew steadily closer to each other as bitter resentment built among us towards our father. Some of the neighbors pitied us. We were laughed at and made fun of at school, but we could do nothing. As a family we learned how to survive within this ugly lifestyle.

Bright Spots Amidst the Ugliness

There were a few bright spots amidst the ugliness we saw a majority of our growing up years. My mother had an only brother whom she hardly ever saw. When he did come to visit with us, we were all very happy to see him, especially my mom. He was a very nice man. He loved us and every visit from him was an enjoyable one. Mom's brother, his wife, and their kids were very special to us. Even though he was also an alcoholic, he was very special in many ways. We all loved him and his family very much the years that followed he became a Christian and serves the lord with gladness.

Our maternal grandmother was a beautiful woman in stature and in person. Her love for us was like a survival antidote. She loved us very much and cared for us like no other family member did. We were her pride and joy. And meant everything to her nothing was too much for her to do for us. Whenever she visited she brought happiness into our lives that lasted for a long time after she left. We cherished her visits; going to her house was even more joyful. She did a lot for us and always made the most delicious foods. She was a very good cook, the best. She always treated us with so much love. She gave us the love we never got from our own parents.

Our grandmother was always a very cheerful person and she made her living by working for the English people as a domestic servant. They liked her and treated her kindly. She would do all their washing, ironing, cooking, cleaning, and caring for their kids. The English kids loved her very much. When we visit her at their bungalows, they would tease us and we teased them right back. They were jealous of us coming to see her she was very special to them. However, I wanted them to know she was our grandmother not theirs.

She always had a kind and loving way of treating everyone she met. An Amazing woman Very special. to us, a woman of great worth. She was born of African heritage. Her Mother was East Indian and her biological father was an African man. The story is told my great-grandmother cheated on her husband and had a secret affair. When my grandmother was born, her mother hid her from her husband because if he saw she was black he would kill the baby. She said to her husband the baby was born with a curse and he could not see her. In those days if a child was born with any deformity that child was considered cursed and could not live with their biological family. The parents would give the child to someone else to care for or let the child die from lack of food and care.

My grandmother's mother whose name was Alice kept her as a baby hidden until she was one year old. She was kept in a cardboard box hidden at all times for her safety. Then when she was a year old she crawled out of the box to where her mother was cooking on an open fire. She pulled a pan of boiling water down on her-self and was badly burned. Her right arm and fingers were so burned they looked disfigured. Her mother kept that a secret, from everyone, and continued to keep her hidden. She made a bandage of wet mud and old rags and wrapped the child's arms to keep them from getting infected.

Though the neighbors were curious about this deformed child, no one found out anything. She grew up with a permanent burn scar. Her right arm never got to grow normal and remained folded against her body with half closed baby fingers. She learned to use her left arm and hand to comb her hair, dress herself, write, cook, sew Do laundry, and everything else she needed to do for herself. She was a hard worker and a talented woman. She became friends with the people she worked for; they love her and showed her appreciation for all that she did for them. Though life was troublesome, she never let things keep her down. She always persevered. She was courageous and strong.

I admired her and she taught me a lot as a young girl growing up. She made sure we had good manners and to be respectful to others, my sister and I were taught to have poise and to be modest in our dress. She would sew us dresses that were well made and very fancy. She loved perfume, jewelry, and nice clothing. She always liked to look glamorous. Whenever she had to attend any social or public events she was the talk of the village because of her poise and elegance.

Most of all I learned to be a great cook from her. I know not that someday I would be like her. I have cherished the memories of her all my life. When she died, I felt the loss very deeply. I've been married and had three kids at the time, of her passing. I felt lonely inside with her gone. She stood by me through the years in difficult times. She really loves us and her love was real. She lives on in all I do and all that I am. I am thankful to God for all she taught me. I'm blessed to have had her in my life growing up there was no one like her. Her love and kindness touched the lives of many of her relatives and neighbors. Her beauty was truly from within!

Chapter 2
A LIVING HELL

At the tender age of fourteen my father decided to get me a husband. During those days your parents found you a husband of their choice. You had little or no say in the matter. At fourteen I was no longer attending school. After the eighth grade, my parents kept me home to learn to keep house, cook, clean, and help take care of the younger siblings. They allowed me to enroll in sewing classes which I loved. Very much I came home one nice sunny day and my mom told me they had found a man for me to marry. I was in shock. I was not happy. I was not ready to get married. This is arranged marriage.

Before I could say anything, my mother said my dad had met a wealthy, well-respected family in another big village. He was arranging for the families to meet in a couple months. I was very unhappy and dreading the day we would meet with this family. When finally I saw the man who would someday be my husband, I was very disappointed. I wanted to run and never stop. I did not say a word to him. He kept looking at me with joy in his eyes. I wanted to die. I was very young and very pretty with long wavy black hair and a neat round face. Everyone said I had a beautiful smile. The boys in the neighborhood teased me just so I would smile for them.

The man's family cooked lots of food for us to eat as they discussed the wedding plans. It was a nice time for everyone but me. I did not like him from the minute I set my eyes on him. He was rich and a drunk. He was not handsome and was not even dressed nicely. *He looks so old*, I said to myself. The last thing I wanted was a drunk for a husband. I had witnessed firsthand what life with a drunk would be. Everyone was eating and drinking and having a good time. I said to myself, *there is no way I am ever marrying this man*. Then fear gripped me as I realized I had no choice in the matter. I had to do what my parents said.

My father gave his approval and set the date. The marriage would take place when I turned seventeen. I was given a stem ring from a mango leaf to show I was arranged in marriage to someone. I wanted to die. I was so sad and unhappy. Life meant nothing to me anymore. My parents knew how I felt, but that never bothered them. My mom had nothing to say. She was always afraid of my dad. We left the home of the so called "arrangement" family, and my siblings started to tease me about him. They knew how I felt and it was a big joke to them. However, it was no laughing matter for me!

When the man's family would come to visit us at our home, I was expected to sit with them and look happy. I sat with them, I never smiled never said a word to any of them. My heart was crippled with fear. *What am I going do?* My father's words were repeated over and over in my head. My dad was only concerned about the large dowry he would get for me. He cared nothing about my happiness. Every time the family visited I wanted to die. I thought of running away from it all, but where would I go? There was no one to save me from this horrible future. Death was the only answer, but that would not happen to me. I was too young. Only old people die, not the young ones. I lived in fear, everyday hoping that wedding day would never come. I held onto that hope. I was always sad, but I could not show it. I kept it all to myself as I did not want my dad to change his mind and move the date up.

As a child I saw my mother being abused by my dad when he was drunk. I did not want that for my future. I had seen this lifestyle of unhappiness, unfaithfulness, and abuse even in the lives of my older cousins who were old enough to marry. Everyone seemed resigned to all that was going on with the drinking and the womanizing of the men even after they married. These men never felt any shame or remorse for their drunken behavior. This was an accepted way of life for the men. I was always bothered by the way they lived their lives. I never understood the acceptance of it. All I knew was I did not want that kind of life when I got married. I did not want to be like those women.

As I waited to be married off to this man, life for me became harder. Every time I thought of my parents' plan for me, fear would grip me. Now I'm in an arranged marriage agreement, I had to undertake more of the household chores of cooking, cleaning, and taking care of my younger siblings in preparation for married life. On my fifteenth birthday my dad reminded me of his promise to this family. My parents also decided to give up working in the sugar cane fields because they felt they needed to be with us more to protect us from getting into any kind of trouble. My father now made his living by selling fish with a little blue van in the surrounding villages. My mother worked for a doctor as a housekeeper for very little money.

This made things even harder on our family financially. We were poor, but we learned to be content with what we had. My grandmother was always giving us anything we needed. We learned to live with what was given to us. We lived in a small village. Everyone knew everyone and in the event of something happening, everyone would come together to offer their help. The people of our village were always generous in times of need no matter what the problem. They were always ready to assist in any way they could. For that we were grateful.

Easter Weekend

Easter weekend was a time when everyone would celebrate with family and friends. The village people would get together to have lots of sporting events, participate in various games, and there were lots of prizes. They even crowned a village queen during this celebration. This was a time of fun and people enjoyed themselves all weekend. My parents had a lot of company over that Saturday. My dad and his friends butchered a pig and sold the meat to friends and neighbors as was the custom at this time of the year. This was a very busy time for all of us. We all had a lot to do, but we never complained as we excitedly looked forward to the day of fun so we could enjoy ourselves amidst the celebration.

We were all so busy we did not notice anything strange or different. We were too caught up in our chores. We wanted to get our daily chores finished and by the end of the day we were exhausted. We all went to bed right after our dinner. We knew we would wake up the next morning to all the fun of that day. We all looked forward to Easter Sunday and all the activities that day would hold. Little did we know that day would never happen for our family this year?

The night before the Easter celebration, something very strange happened to me. We lived in a small house. My only sister and I shared a bed in the front bedroom and four of my brothers shared the room next to ours on the upper level of our house. My parents slept downstairs in one bedroom and my two other brothers slept in the second bedroom in the lower part of our house. It was the middle of the night and everyone was asleep when I suddenly woke up with a strange feeling. I felt as if I was not in my bed. It was a very unusual feeling. I felt frighten. I looked down at the foot of our bed and standing there was a figure of a young girl who looked like one of my girl cousins. I started to shake in fear.

I asked this girl what she doing here. She did not answer so I repeated my question. The doors were closed so I did not know how she could have gotten in. When I asked her again, she gave me an ugly sort of smile and in that moment she jumped up and entered into my body. I was terrified. I felt as if I was choking. I could feel pain in my throat so I started to scream out loud. I screamed louder and louder until my sister woke up. She started screaming even though she did not know what had happened to me or what I had seen.

Then my four brothers came running in thinking someone had come in to attack us. My parents ran into the room wondering why I was screaming. As I tried to tell them what I had seen, my father instantly knew something evil had frightened me. He did what he knew to do to ward off evil. He began to say his Hindu prayers over me. My mother tried to comfort me, but my screams were so loud the neighbors woke up and were calling out to find out what had happened to me. My dad stopped praying and told them I had seen something that frightened me. The villagers knew it was not good by the sound of the screams.

As my parents were trying to calm me down, this thing that had entered me started beating me all over my face and body. My parents and siblings could see the welts popping up on my face and body, but no one could understand what was happening. Then I fainted and began to see myself tie up to a tree with fire all around me. I was being burned and beaten alive. I was screaming for my life, but no one heard me. No one came to my rescue. Wherever I was in my spirit, this was what was happening to me even in the physical. My family could not see my torture. All they could see were the welts continuing to show up on me. My appearance began to change from a very pretty to an ugly deformed person.

I must have screamed for a couple hours. Finally, in the wee hours of the morning, I fell into a deep sleep. When I awoke the next morning everyone was sleeping on the bed. My mother got up and quickly took bed sheets and covered all the mirrors in the house. She did not want me to see myself. I began to move in and out of consciousness. I was very weak and my hands and feet would not stop shaking. I was confused about what had taken place that night. I asked my family what had happened and they told me I was very sick. My mom told us they did not know what happen to me they were taking me to the doctor. Then I asked her why all the mirrors were covered and she said they did not want me to see myself because something bad had happened to me during the night. My sister said it was like I had changed into a different person.

I kept feeling as if something was stuck in my throat. My siblings just stared at me and would not talk to me as if they were afraid of me. Every time they looked at me they started crying. The neighbors kept coming over and asking my parents about me. They talked among themselves, but I could not hear what they saying. I got more and more scared and confused. What had happened to me? That morning my dad called over to his mother and two younger brothers. He talked with them about what might have happened to me. He did not know what to do about me. He was advised by family and friends to take me to a doctor so they would have an idea of what might have happened.

Unnatural Causes

After examining me, the doctor gave my parents some kind of medication to help me sleep. He told them I had lost my mind and recommended confining me to a mental institution for treatment as he could not treat me for this condition. My father became very angry, told the doctor off, and took me home. My parents had to decide what to do with me. They both knew this sickness was not of natural causes and decided to seek spiritual help from my father's Hindu priest. Little did they realize this would be a battle that would last for months?

All the way home from the doctor's my body was further marred by the never ending beatings from the demons spirits. The screams were hideous and hard for my parents to listen to as they drove home with me. Everyone at home was waiting to hear what the doctor had to say. My father decided if they did not move fast I would die from this thing. He told everyone this was not natural sickness so his relatives and all the people in the village gave them advice as to what to do and where to go for help. My siblings watched me and wondered to themselves what would become of me. Doubts and fear filled their little hearts. They felt sorry for me and cried every day. I could only imagine what they must have been feeling at that moment and the terror that must have gripped their young hearts as they saw their sister turn into this "other person."

I lost my mind and all consciousness of who I was or where I was. All reality was gone and I had no ability to do anything for myself. All was left of me was a screaming young girl who was not able to explain herself or her feelings. I was in a world of darkness and pain. I did not know where I was and had no control over what was happening to me. No one could understand me. No one had any answers that could bring comfort to my parents. My mom and sister had to do all my personal care. They bathed, dressed, and even fed me. This was extremely difficult for them.

Days went by and things got worse instead of better so they made a decision to try spiritual methods. Off they went to the Hindu priest to see what help he could offer. After some

A Living Hell

Hindu prayers and chants, a couple of his spiritual baths, a small sacrifice to his gods, he then told them someone had invoked some evil spirits and sent them to kill me. I was a sacrifice of death he told them and gave them the name of the person who did this to me. He then gave them some secrets sacraments for me to wear around my neck and waist as protection from the spirits trying to kill me. He warned my parents that these evil spirits were living inside me and if they didn't come out they would lose me. They had to move fast or I could die. This is horrible for them.

I can only imagine what my parents must have felt when they heard all of this. They did what he said and the screams would cease for a short time. I would be quiet and it looked as if I was better, but would last only a few days. Then they would take me back to the Hindu priest. Every time he gave them a solution, his method failed. They kept trying over and over again. I had stopped eating regular foods and asked for only plain bread and water. This was what the demons wanted to eat. The voice that spoke from me was not me. Though it sounded like my voice, it was controlled by the demon spirits living in me. Whatever the demons wanted to eat or drink, it was fed to me. At times very strange things would be spoken from my mouth by these demons. Eventually nine demons took full control of my body. My life was not mine any more. As a human being I had died. I was physically alive yet I was dead. My hands and feet did weird things, the screams continued to get louder and scarier. My face was so black and ugly I was no longer recognizable to my family.

My parents continued to do what had to be done to keep me alive, but after weeks of doing everything they could think of, there was no change in my condition. They became very discouraged as time and time again they would take me to every kind of priest and priestess of every different religion they could think of to seek help for me. One priestess said they had to leave me with her. So they left me and she practiced all her sacrificial ceremonies on me for many days. She made different religious offerings to all the gods she knew. She really worked hard on me. She was young just as I was and had super spiritual powers to control evil spirits.

She would sacrifice chickens as a blood offering to the spirits in the middle of the night. Then she would take cloves and place them on me and cast a spell so the spirits will come out of me. Those cloves would jump up and down as if they were alive and jump around the room. She would catch them and place them in a bottle of alcohol to kill them. At times the spirit that came out of me would stick to my body and she had to pinch deep into my flesh to get them out of me. She even cut into my skin to get them out. There were a lot of them and she had to catch them all. She could not let even one get away from her for fear they would go into someone else. She had to be very careful in what she was doing. For a few days she was successful, but eventually she failed just like all the others before her. She got tired of me and told my parents to come and take me home telling them that what was on me was too strong for her.

Again all was in vain. There were times certain things worked for a day or two and then I would fall back into the

same madness again. No one had the answer to wha
to end this horror. Finally someone told them to try the v(
priest. So off they went and this priest gave me a necklace
made of garlic to wear around my neck and a string of garlic
to wear around my waist. My body was covered with garlic.
By the time I got home, those things had come alive and were
choking me and trying to kill me. My parents took me back
to the voodoo priest who told my dad to bring him a pig and
money to offer to the demon gods and I would be better in no
time. Desperate, my dad took the pig to this priest to offer for
my life. The pig was offered to the demon gods and the blood
of the pig was rubbed all over me as the voodoo priest recited
his chants and spells.

For a few days it seemed to work and I was quiet, but soon everything started again. My parents went back to the voodoo priest as he was able to control the demons and quiet them down again, but told them he did not have the power to get them out of me and sent them to another voodoo priest. When one priest could not control what was happening to me, they would send us to another voodoo priest and another one and so on. My parents kept going from one place to another for months. I got worse as these people tried all their black magic spells and performed ceremony after ceremony. Not one of them was strong enough to cast these demons out of my body.

By now my parents were nearly out of money and started to lose hope for me. The hardship they had to endure was unbearable. All the running from place to place kept them from working. They were struggling for money and my siblings were neglected, because all of their time was spent on trying to find a healing for me day after day, night after night. We traveled for many miles from village to village just to get the best kind of help there was for me. Whatever advice, counsel or method of any kind they were given, my parents would do. The priests, priestesses, and witch doctors did all kinds of magic spells. My parents were so desperate; they did whatever was asked of them.

One witch doctor beat me with a broom made of coconut palm leaves and even bit my stomach to try and get the demons out of me. This went on for weeks as he told my parents it was the only thing left to do. My parents watched in horror as all that was being done to me. This witch doctor even cut parches of hair from my head. I had huge bald sports on my head making me look uglier and crazier than ever. I must have been a sight to look at! No wonder my siblings were afraid of me!

From Beauty to a Beast

My body became lifeless from all the ugly things being done to me by all of these people. After months of trying and waiting, my parents got to the point of giving up. I had become blind and could not speak. I had grown long finger nails and toe nails that looked like claws. My face was twisted and I had long black ugly hair with bald spots all over my head. I was a crazy animal, screaming and howling in such a frightful way people were scared to come to visit. Neighbors and villagers stopped coming. The money had run out, and they started to give up hope of me ever getting out of this evil hold except through death.

Eventually someone mentioned talking to the Catholic priest. With no hope left, they took me to the Catholic Church. The priest looked at me and told them he did not know how he should handle me, but he would pray over me. He gave them a bottle of holy water and a rosary. I had to wear the rosary around my neck and they were to sprinkle the holy water on me three times a day. He also gave them a prayer to say for me. He told them to bring me back and he would pray for me again. They carried me to the priest to be prayed for again and again. He was scared of me and what I looked like, and after a few weeks he told them it was no use. He told them I would never get better and never be normal again.

That was the last straw for my poor parents. There was nothing more they could do for me after months and months of trying. They felt helpless and alone and felt time was running out for me. They had to come to the reality I was going to die a slow, painful, ugly death and there was nothing more they could do for me. The overwhelming agony they had to live with filled them with anger and hate. My father wanted to kill the person who brought this on me. Every day was a living hell for them. The neighbors were always trying to keep my father calm. He was a man full of rage and was not afraid of anyone. He did not care if he lived or died. Somehow the people in the village were able to keep him under control by constantly talking to him. There were days he would not eat and they cared for him.

My parents were so very worried for me. This was a nightmare that would not come to an end. The future was so grim and uncertain for my family. They not only had to try to get help for my deliverance, they had to deal with all the other things that were happening with my siblings. They all lived in fear as the manifestations of demons and demon activities took place in the home. Furniture would move from the room without anyone moving it. Doors would open all by themselves. My siblings would hear voices calling them and there were strange noises at all hours of the day or night. They would see shadows moving around when there was no one else in the house. Often my siblings would become so scared they would scream and run out the house.

My siblings could only watch in horror as all these things happened all around them. This was terrifying for them since they were often alone. They lived in fear for their own lives. No one would come to be with them or comfort them either. The relatives and neighbors were so scared they all stayed away from our house and wanted nothing to do with our family. They all went about living their lives and taking care of their families while my siblings were left unattended. Since no one came to take care of them, they learned how to cook and feed themselves.

Once my parents realized all the frightful and evil things that now surround us in the home, they invited the priests to come to the house to perform religious ceremonies and say prayers. It would stop for a short time; this was a horrible torment for them. Knowing their other children was left unattended so much of the time. Many times all of my siblings would go with my parents on these trips to the voodoo priests and priestesses. They witnessed some of the things done to me to help me be free from all the torment. One can only imagine what they were thinking as they watched in horror as these people used their mystical magic spells and powers trying to cast out the demons in me. These voodoo priests and priestesses often chanted as they danced and spun around like crazy people. This was a lot of superstitions my family watched in great fear, but they never gave up trying.

Only God knows how they got through all this and taught themselves to be brave and strong. My young, innocent siblings were forced to pay a bitter price for something no one had control of or had done to bring this on our family. On top of that, our family was the talk of the village. The neighbors were always giving advice. Soon there was no hope left even in the village people. This was a very horrific thing for my family, our friends, and neighbors to experience. All that time my life was slipping away slowly right before their eyes.

I was unaware of all that was taking place with me. I was always unconscious, never knowing myself or my surroundings. I was unable to see or hear or even touch my family. It was devastating to them as they tried to talk to me, and heard the demons respond using my voice if there was any response at all. At times they told me they could hardly tell the difference because the demon voice was so like my own voice.

Preparing for the End

My family continued to do all they could to keep me alive. They kept feeding me whatever I would ask for to eat and drink, but in fact they were feeding the demons in me. They just wanted to make sure I did not starve. They also made sure that I was always clean and smelled good. My mom never let me remain dirty or smelly. When people have these demons they often smell stinky and have a dirty look. My hair would not stay combed, but they tried as much as they could. As hope waned, they would draw strength from anyone who showed some concern for them and for my life. It was important to them to hold on to hope, believing somehow there was an answer or something out there for them to do for me if they were just persistent. Whatever it took they were willing to pay the price, but soon they felt they were fighting a losing battle.

The days and nights were long and hard for them. The turmoil never seemed to end. This was now their life and there seemed to be no way out. So they live from day to day. Finally, my dad had to sell the house we lived in. This was the only possession he had. We had to move out of that village to start over in another place. Our house was sold to one of my dad's brothers who lived across the street from us and had witnessed everything we had been through. This was not easy for my dad to do, but he had to find a way to survive. He had to provide for and take care of his family. After a while they found an apartment to rent and went from owning their own house to renting an apartment.

Their life was a mess all because of what had happened to me. The most painful thing for them was to watch me suffer and not able to help me. Months had gone by and the decision was made to stop all the unsuccessful treatments. They knew my life would be over soon, they felt they had run out of options. I would die and it looked like it was going to happen very soon. No parent should have to endure this kind of intense sadness with their children. My parents were forced to watch their child suffer every day, realizing there was nothing more they could do to make that suffering go away. The nightmare held them captive they could not eat or drink or experience a good night's sleep.

Finally, my dad told everyone they would have to start to prepare for my funeral. It was no use anymore. Karma was never going to get better and they just had to wait for my death. They started to mourn my loss while I was still living because of the torment and agony they saw surrounding me. All hope was gone; it was time to prepare for the end.

Chapter 3
BUT GOD

Just when everything seemed hopeless, somehow, someone told my dad about a church where Jesus was being preached and Jesus could help me. By now my dad did not want to hear about anything else that might help. He was beyond exhausted and tired of all those other things that did not work. He had given up hope and felt, what is the use? It is not going to help. There was no one who could help us.

He had given up and so had my mom. All hope was gone from them, but all was not lost. My grandmother used all her influence to convince them to give me this one last chance. She kept begging and begging. She told my dad I was going to die anyway so what did he have to lose by taking me to that church. It would be the decent thing to do, and then they could say they had tried everything there was to help. She kept on pleading with him to at least give this church a try and see what they could do. She refuge to give up trying until she convinced him to change his mind. It took a few weeks, and then he finally agreed to make one last try. He told my mom they were wasting their time, but he would go to the church and give this one a last effort to make sure they had tried everything.

Jesus said ..."with men this is impossible; but with "God all things are possible'... Matthew 19: 26

One Last Try

It was a bright sunny Thursday morning. The whole family got up early, dressed, and got ready to go with me to this full gospel church. My dad had a little old blue van which he used to sell his fish in the villages. This was the only transportation we had so with the help of neighbors, they got me in the van and off to the church we went.

There was a church service called Mountain Movers going on at the church. It was a deliverance meeting for people who needed to be healed from any kind of disease or oppression. There were people there who had all kinds of specials needs in their lives such as oppression and demon possession like me, there were the physically ill, and even those that needed healing in their marriages. Those who had suggested we come had reported they had seen many miracles at these services.

We arrived at the church around nine am. And were greeted. by the ushers at the door. My dad explained to them what's going on with me they offered to help get me out of the van and into the church. I could not walk they had to carry me. It took ten men to lift me out and carry me because I was kicking and fighting. I screamed loud hideous screams as they carried me. These ushers had never seen anything like this before in their lives. When the people in the church saw me and heard me, they knew instantly. I was a demon possess girl. Many of them were scared of me. I can hardly imagine what I must have looked like and how my poor parents felt at that moment. Im sure they were very embarrassed, but at the same time they wanted healing for their daughter.

Once I was in the church, the drama began to unfold. I was taken to the front row of pews in the church with my whole family. As soon as the singing started, my body began to do strange things. My hands and feet started to fold up as if someone were tying me up. I stared as one does that is blind. Though I could not talk. the screams kept coming from inside me. Then the minister began to preach from the Holy Bible. As he preached about the miracles that Jesus had done, the demon manifestations got very disruptive. I was placed on the floor so I would not fall off the pew and hurt myself. I immediately started wiggling like a snake between the pews and howling like a wild animal. People had to move from where they were sitting to get safely away from me.

Though the ushers and my parents were doing their best to keep me under control, it was no use. The manifestations were so strong these demons would say crazy things about how they came to kill me and they were not leaving me. They declared they were sent to do this. They bragged about how they were living in my tummy. I was as big a pregnant woman. These were evil, powerful demons determined to take my life.

After the minister finished preaching, he came to lay his hands on me and to pray for me as was the custom in Pentecostal churches. I immediately got quiet as he continues to command the demons to get out of me. They started to manifest again and told him they were not leaving me. They talked back to him and even threaten him. When he prayed they became very vicious, cursed, and screamed the screams of death. Sometimes they got tired and remained quiet in my body then I would start screaming. This was frightful to many of the people. These spirits even told him their names, where they came from, and where they lived when the host body dies.

These demons did not want to leave without me. Their purpose was to take my life and they were not giving up. My parents took me back every day for the next couple of weeks. There were times I would be placed in a locked prayer room with praying people because this kind of demonic manifestation was very disruptive during the services. One day as I was in the prayer room with people praying, the demon got up, rushed to the door, and broke the lock. The people in the room with me tried to hold on to me, but I got loose and ran out. They were joined by the church ushers who caught me and took me back to the prayer room fighting and kicking.

When there were no visible signs of release, the minister told my family to take me to the front row of pews in the church. Nothing happened during the singing, but when the minister begins to preach, I suddenly got up and ran full force towards the front door. I was so fast no one could stop me. As I reached to the door, the senior minister was just entering the church building. As he came in the door, I ran head on into him. My head hit him as if I had run into a concrete wall. I fell to the floor with a loud bang. Immediately the preaching stopped and everyone got instantly silent. And assumed I was dead and did not know what to do. I had actually been knocked unconscious and remained that way for a couple hours. These Christian people started praying for me to bring me back to life. Some were crying with my family, especially my mom who screamed out loud thinking this was the end.

The minister encouraged them to keep on praying as this was only a trick from the demons. He was right. Being a very spiritual. Man and full of the wisdom. Of God. Was highly respected by all the followers of his church they prayed that I would open my eyes. My body was cold, I've stopped breathing, and my teeth were locked so tight they could not force my mouth open to get air to breathe. A couple of hours later I did wake up. These demons were so powerful. They would do anything to get attention and distract the church service. Only the power of God could deliver me from this ugly mess.

After a couple of weeks, my dad got fed up and told my mom they were wasting their time again. This church was like all the others and could not help me. He got up and angrily dragged me out of the church right in front of the minister and all the people. My mom and the people of the congregation followed, pleading with him not to do this and not to give up. A few of the men helped him get me into the blue van. He did not respond. He just drove off once all of us were in the van. I cannot imagine what a day that must have been for my mom and siblings. No one said a word, afraid of what my dad might do when they arrived home. When we did get home, my dad announced to everyone it was over and I would soon die. He instructed everyone to get ready and to plan for my funeral.

Fear gripped the hearts of my family, relatives, and the villagers. They had heard this said about me many times before, but now it seemed this was really going to happen.

My dad did not understand what it is to have faith in an unseen and unknown God. All his life all he had ever known was his Hindu prayers and chants. After all they had been through and everything they had tired, he was so angry and frustrated that he threatened to kill anyone who tried to come near me to try and help me get better. He had had enough promises and was at the end of his rope. He just could not handle anymore. It was over for him. He needed to stop his family's suffering. All hope was truly gone for good. I became like the living dead to them.

A week went by and I remained pretty quiet. The screams were still happening, but not very often. My grandmother came to see me and told my dad not to give up without a fight. She had a very powerful way pleading with him every day to go back to the church and allow the power of God to free me from this strong demonic power. This took another week for her to get through to him. She convinced him he had to believe his Karma would live. He eventually changed his mind. When we did arrive at the church the next week everyone was surprised to see us. This time it would be a battle to the end for my life.

A Faith-filled Fight for Life.   *"Have Faith in God". Mark 11:22*

This would be a faith-filled fight for my life. The minister knew it and encouraged the people in the church to keep on praying. They never gave up. These were some brave people.

They read the words from the Holy Bible out loud and encouraged my family that I would be delivered and would live. They taught them to have faith in God. These people did their best to bring hope to my family. After a couple of hours, the minister and the elders finished praying for me and told them to take me home.

As we left for home, my parents were not sure what to expect. I remained very quiet all the way home. There were no screams and no more manifestations. They knew something was different, but did not understand it. When we got home, I was carried into the house. Not a word came from me. My family was not sure what to do now. I was good for a week. Just when they thought this was over for them, one night while everyone was asleep, out came a very loud scream.

Though this was not new to them, when they rushed to my side this time it was different. My mom got out the Bible and started to read out loud from it. And things got quiet and they began to recognize the power that entered the room as my mother read the words of Bible. From then on, whenever this would happen, my mother would read the Bible out loud. She realized it gave her power over these spirits. My entire family begins to build faith in the words of the Bible. We also kept on going to the church in spite of the sometimes embarrassing evil manifestations. No matter what they were feeling or what people were saying about them, my parents began to turn their lives around. We attended the church regularly as a family.

After a few months the minister admonished the congregation to fast and pray for not only my deliverance, but for all the sick and oppressed in the congregation. The power of fasting and prayer of these faithful people was too strong for these demons. The name of Jesus was powerful and the demons were very afraid of that name. People were healed and delivered by His great name. As they witnessed the power of the name of Jesus, my parents started to trust this name and this new God they had found.

The minister had a meeting with my family. and they told him all that had happened with me before coming to the church. He encouraged them and gave them the assurance if they would hold on, have faith, and believe in God a miracle would happen someday soon. He did not know how soon. He knew I would be made free and live a very long life. He prayed with our entire family and for the first time they felt truly comforted. He advised them to keep reading the Holy Bible daily; he gives my parents scriptures to read to help as they continue pray for me. This was the first time they were told to do something for me that did not cost them any money. All the services were free and these church people were very nice and friendly to them. The presence of God was truly felt in this church. The atmosphere was peaceful as they felt the love of the people. This was a new experience for them.

A Life Changing Decision

My parents made a definite decision to bring me to church regularly. They started to see little signs of healing. At times I would be conscious and confused. They just told me I had been very sick though no explanation was given to me as what kind of sickness. I had, I was experiencing feelings that were confusing to me. I could actually talk for myself. When I did my family looked at me in surprise. I did not know at the time they could not tell the difference in my voice and that of the demons. I did not understand why my family did not tell me anything about what was going on as this began to happen. I asked questions about what happened to me and everyone looked at me strangely, no one would answer my questions.

At times I would feel like I'm in a daze and my head was spinning with confusion. As time went on, they continued to bring me to this church and many other full gospel churches where there was any kind of healing service. They were encouraged to take a step forward, but came to a point where they could see there was something holding them captive. They could not understand what it was or why they never felt the freedom other people around them seemed to be experiencing. Finally, they sought counsel from the minister as to what they needed to do to achieve this freedom.

One of the things he told them to do was to get rid of all the false gods we had in our house. They needed to turn away from Hinduism and turn to the one true God. Everything that had been given to them by the Hindu priest, all the voodoo priests and priestesses, and all the black magic stuff had to be destroyed. They had to clean out the entire house from all these other so called spiritual methods. Everything had to be burned. Nothing was to be hidden or saved. This was the only way to truly be free. They had to make a complete turn a around. There could be no compromise. They had to believe only in the one true God.

In their amazement. They did not hesitate. They were ready to make whatever changes were necessary in their lives no

But God

matter what the cost. It was the right time for them to do something new and completely different. The minister also spoke with them more about the Holy Bible, explained all about faith in God, and the promises He had given to heal and deliver the sick. All they had to do was just to believe in God and trust in Him for me as I could not do that for myself. He told them if they would have faith and believe in God, I would be healed, made whole, and I would live. After their counseling session, my parents decided to do as he had spoken them.

My father led the family as they did as they were told. They gathered all the gods, all the magic potions, and spiritual methods they had, and had a bon fire. They burned all that was evil. Not one thing was forgotten or left out. My father made sure of that though it was a bit hard for him since from childhood all he had known was the Hindu faith. He grew up in the Hindu belief and now he had to give it up and let it go, all for the sake of his child's life. He had to tell his mother and two brothers what he had to do and that he was going to become a Christian. When one turns from the Hindu religion they become an outcast of that family. My father suffered that from his family as he chose to make a decision that would change everyone's lives forever. He was the first in his generation to become a born again Christian, all because of me.

He led my mom and my siblings to turn their lives around and turn to the Christian faith. They gave up the life they used to live and began to live a new life in Jesus Christ. They accepted this new life and learned about a God they never knew existed but had still loved them. This God had sent His only Son to die for them just to prove His love for them. This was new to them. Hearing this for the first time brought a life of change and understanding of a God that was powerful enough to do anything for them and it cost them nothing. They did not have to pay any money to learn all this which really surprised my dad.

In a very short period of time things became very different for them. My family learned a whole new way of life and how to pray together. The learned to read the Holy Bible, a book that was so different yet so meaningful and comforting to the whole family. My family's obedience paid off. Though I was still possessed, they now had a new method of how to handle me. Whenever there was a manifestation, they would begin to pray and read the Holy Bible out loud. They were consistent in doing this for me and soon they began to notice the difference every time they did so. They began to make new friends and adjust to living a Christian life. They attended church more often and continued to bring me with them. They watched me hoping that soon all this would end.

Hold On for the Miracle

"Now faith is the substance of things hoped for the evidence of things not seen". Hebrews 11:1

As time went by all was not what my father expected. Many months went by and again he was not able to cope with the changes in his life without seeing a big change in mine. He got fed up and started to complain to my mother how all these new changes were a waste of time. Discouragement set in and he got frustrated. He felt things were moving too slow for him in the church. He wanted me to be instantly healed. He was at the point of giving up for good, this time my family stood up to him. He soon realized they were serious now more than ever before. He had no choice but to humble him-self and surrender just for me.

The church people remained faithful in fasting and praying for our family and my deliverance. The battle raged stronger, and the people were determined to win this fight for my life. They try their very best to help my family hold on to faith in God's Word. As they stood strong for me. They could not resist the power and grace of God. My family did not want me to die an ugly death so with all their might and strength, they put all their belief in this new God they had found. Without knowing for sure what the outcome would be, they held on stronger than ever.

Suddenly, one day while the congregation was praying for me, a miracle happened. My hands and feet just stretch out as if someone was pulling them straight. My skin color looks a bit lighter. Right then these people knew something good had happened. Soon after I started to vomit and out came some foul smelling stuff. It stunk terribly and must have been the evil spirits that were living inside me coming out. They came out very slowly, one at a time. My hair did not got all loose and wild. It remained combed for a long time which was another sign something was changing slowly with me.

From then on there were more little signs of behavioral changes that showed things were happening. In another church service my body was lying flat on the floor as if I was asleep during the preaching. As the minister kept on preaching, I suddenly started screaming and coughing uncontrollably.

This was no ordinary cough. I was choking like something was trying to get out of my throat. The more I coughed the worse it got. At times I could not breathe. Then I began to vomit more stinky stuff that was horrible and foul smelling. These were like little balls that dissipated when I spew them up. Time after time this would happen and then I would feel better. This kind of behavior began to happen so often that soon it became normal to everyone who was praying for me. This was the only way these things could get out of me. One by one they were being cast out of my body. These faith filled Christian people continued praying. They never gave up on me or my family. This continued for a couple more months. All these things were happenings as signs I would soon be free from all possession. My family kept their faith in God hoping someday soon this will be over for me and for them.

Chapter 4
ALL THINGS NEW

"Therefore if any man be in Christ, he is a new creature: old things are pass away: behold all things are become new". 2 Corinthians 5:17

One Sunday night we were all in church. As the service got started I felt a strange feeling. Came over me somehow. I became conscious of my surroundings. It was as if I woke up and was sitting in a strange place with no idea how I had gotten there. Everything was strange. The singing was new to me. I had never heard the songs they were singing before. I've never been in this huge building before and did not recognize any of the people around me. I did not know where I was or what was going on. I ask myself.

What is this place? Where am I? What is happening to me? Is this a dream? Am I awake? Am I dead and in the next world? Nothing made any sense to me. I did not know if I was even real. As I looked around me, I realized my sister was sitting next to me. I asked her where we at, why we here, and who are all these people sitting around me. She said to me we are in a church. Then she explained I had been sick and our parents had been bringing me here to help me get better. When I asked her what was wrong with me, she started to cry. I did not say another word. My parents were sitting close to us just to make sure I did not act up again. My sis turned to quietly tell my parents what I had said. They already knew. Since they kept their eyes constant on me.

In fact every eye in the whole church was on me. I had remained quiet since we had arrived at the church which was very unusual. The singing continued as I looked around at the people. Everyone was standing but me. My feet and hands felt kind of weird. In fact my entire body felt weird. I made an attempt to stand up and as I did everyone began to move away from me except my family. I don't know how long it took me, but I finally stood up. At that instant something very strange happened to me. I don't know how long I've had been standing, when all of a sudden someone or something grab my left arm and with full force pulled me from where I was standing and hurled me towards the church altar.

People got scared when they saw me walking to the altar. All eyes were on me as I reached the altar; I felt a deep sharp pain running through my head as if someone had cut my head open. The pain was unbearable I screamed so loud with every ounce of breath I had. It was very frightening to me. While screaming I fell to the floor unconscious. I don't know how long I must have laid there or what happened during that time, but one thing was sure, something was happening. The entire church continues to pray out loud for my deliverance. This was what everyone was waiting and believing to see happen, this miracle of faith from God.

I laid there unconscious for maybe an hour or two. When I woke up I was in a daze and very confused. I was not sure what had happened to me. I finally was able to fully open my eyes.

The minister looked directly at me and shouted, "What is your name?"

With the little strength I had, I answered in a very faint voice, "My name is Karma."

He asked me several more times what my name was and I kept repeating, "My name is Karma,"

Finally, he leaned over pulled me up off the floor, and sat me on the pew. He had to make sure it was me and not the demons talking. Every other time he had asked me my name before today, they would answer him with their evil names. This time when I answered with my own name, all the people started to shout praises to God and kept on singing. Some of them were praying out loud and some were even crying. My family members were all crying tears of joy I was not dead.

The minister said to me, "Say, 'Thank you Jesus.'"

I did as he told me. Then he told me to repeat the name of Jesus several more times. I did all that he asked me to do.

Then one more time he asked me, "What is your name?"

I shouted, "Karma! My name is Karma!"

Everyone was overjoyed! They could not stop rejoicing over me and this big victory in my life. They kept going on and on praising God as I looked around for my family. I could not understand why everyone was so excited. When I finally saw my family, I was so happy to see them.

Healed and Whole

"But Jesus turned him about. And when he saw her He said. Daughter be of good comfort: thy faith hath made thee whole": Matthew 9:22

My family faith in God for me was proof this God is real. I was told I had been delivered from all the demons that had possessed me for so long. I was now free, healed, and made whole! This is a great miracle I'm alive. They had waited for so long for this miracle of life. All the agony, pain, and suffering were finally over! This was a time of new life for everyone who had stood with my family for so long!

The congregation continued to rejoice over my deliverance. This was new and very confusing to me. I really could not comprehend all that had gone on with me over the past several months. All I really knew at the time was my body felt very light. My vision was somewhat different. I did not realize I had not seen light for a long time. Even though for months my eyes had been open, I was blind and living in total darkness. At first I had no physical feelings of my own. Then suddenly, I had them all back. I could feel my hands, arms, and legs and move them for myself. I was coming back to life.

I was now a whole new person, a brand new human being. Everyone and everything around me was new. I could not explain all that was happening as my eyes adjusted to the light. I heard voices all around me. I looked around to see what was going on. I heard phrases like, "Karma has been delivered.

Karma has been made whole. She lives by the power of God. Karma is back. She has opened her eyes. She will live. She is free from those demons that had her bound for so long. No more suffering for her anymore. No more torment, no more screams from her. At last her deliverance is here. This is a new beginning for her and her family. What a happy time for everyone!"

Many were reading the Bible out loud. The name of Jesus was heard constantly. There were lots of people shouting, "Thank you, Jesus," and "Praise the Lord." This was a spiritual victory party. The words of prayer had now become words of praise. Everyone was coming up to me and greeting me. They were giving me scriptures to read and even praying for me. There was great joy and happiness on their faces. Their joy shone like lights all around me. Happy voices praising God came to my ears as I was covered with all this newness of life. I was experiencing a whole new world, but did not understand any of it. I did not know how to respond to all this or what to do. I really felt like I was in a dream. Was I really in a church full of people? Was I really surrounded by love and warmth? If this was real what was I supposed to do now?

The New Me

"As the father hath loved me" So have I loved you continue ye in my love." John 15:9

This is new to me having someone saying to me a God I don't know loved me. I could not understand. What kind of life was I to have now? What about my family? What does all this mean to me now that I was awake and free? How was I going to live? Was I the same person, the same Karma I was before all this happened? I was very messed up and confused. I needed a mirror to look at myself to see if I was real. It was too much for me to figure out while all the rejoicing was going on all around me.

Suddenly my confusion was replaced with another strange feeling inside me. It was a feeling of rest. I never before felt anything like this. It felt like a bubble in my stomach. There was a feeling of joy and of peace bubbling up inside of me. I felt alive this was a good feeling! I did not want these feelings to ever leave me. These were the best feelings I had ever felt! This was the new me and I liked it!

We must have stayed until midnight at the church just to be sure that nothing would try and possess me again. This time there were no tricks from the demons as there had been in the past. This was for real this time! We had the victory! The minister counseled with my family, prayed with us, and advised them to take me home. Soon afterwards people started to leave for their homes.

I suddenly realized I was very hungry. I felt I had not eaten food in months. As if I had been starved. This hunger was not the usual hunger, this was starvation. I was exhausted. I had no strength, no energy, and I was mentally weak. I could barely remember what food tasted like. It had been months since my body had tasted real food. I had basically survived only on bread and water. The demons made their demands and my family did just that to keep me alive.

When we left the church, we drove to our new home. My family had moved from a house to an apartment in another village while I was unaware of what was going and around me. As I walked into the apartment, everything seemed so odd to me. It was crowded and cluttered, but our family of ten and my grandmother were comfortable and happy to be together. We had running water in the house which was nice. We did not have to go to the standpipe in the village to fetch clean water for our needs. Everything was so different; I felt I was in another dream. We all sat down to eat. I ate and ate while my siblings stared at me as if they had never seen me before. They were very careful what they said around me. I just wanted to cry, but I was so hungry, I just sat there and ate like one who had been starved for months.

Then I went to bed. I slept without waking up until the next morning. My parents stayed awake to make sure I was alright. And nothing happened to me while I slept. The next morning I awoke with the ability to do things for myself. My body was very weak, my voice was real and my eyes sight had fully returned. I looked in the mirror and saw I was beautiful. I could do stuff for myself. My new life was amazing. Seems as if I had died and come back to life.

Life Begins Anew

"Peace I leave with you, my peace I give unto you not as the world giveth give I unto you let not your heart be troubled neither let it be afraid." John 14:27

Karma

My parents started to function in a more normal way in their lives. My dad went back to work selling fish in his little blue van. My mom went back to work for the doctor as a house keeper. she was given the time off me to care for me as long as it took, and they were glad she had come back to work for them. There was peace in our home. As for me, I was not afraid of anything. I had a lot of catching up to do. I had to learn about this new God and the Holy Bible. All this was a mystery to me.

My family was the same, but our lives had been drastically changed. They told me I would now have to read the Bible, pray every day, and attend church so the demons would not come back on me. This was my only protection. They were afraid of me being re-possessed. I was willing to do whatever I was told to avoid this ever happening. They lived in fear for me hoping this never happens to me again. I always felt if ever this should happen again I would surely die.

My only hope now is to learn more about this God and keep close to Him so I would be safe. I was given a Bible of my own. At first I did not know what to read or where to start. I was told to just read the book of john. All that mattered was realizing the Holy Bible was now part of my new life. I was very determined to learn everything there was to know. About my new God. As I began to read more and more, I liked what I was reading. As I continued to read, I felt a holy presence within me and around me as if an angel was guarding me and my family. This was very assuring and brought peace instead of fear into my life. I began to learn about the power of this magnificent God who so powerful delivered me saved my life and changed my family. I realized I was a living testimony of His power. We had a peace we never had before.

We continued to attend church. Whenever there was a service we would be there. We went on weekdays and Sundays. There was so much joy every time we attended church. I loved this new way of living. Everything had meaning. We had new friends and met a lot of nice people. The songs they sang had so much joy, the minister and the people loved us. This was a new world for us. A new beginning that we would all have to live. We did though it was not without a lot of struggles along the way.

We were constantly criticized by our relatives who tried to discourage us and make us turn back to the Hindu belief. This was particularly hard for my dad since he could not read or write English. He was happy I had gotten my life back, but was torn between choosing a new religion and his relatives. Through his life all he's ever known was his belief in Hinduism. Now he has to learn about the new God that saved me and gave me life. This was not easy for him. He literally had given up his family to make this drastic change in his life.

My mom did not have as difficult a time as my dad did. She knew how to read and write so she kept encouraging everyone of us by reading the Holy Bible out loud to us daily. My grandmother did as well. They were just so happy. My siblings were glad I was alive and life was normal and peaceful again. They could go to school regularly without any fear of losing me. My presence was important to them. We ate, played, and laughed together. This was wonderful to just be happy as a family and not have to worry about me or feed me. The fear that gripped them so often was no longer there. This was all behind them now. New Life of Gods peaces now fill everyone.

This was a miracle for our whole family, one we will cherish forever. When I heard they had experience and been through, I would say they loved me and cared about me very much. They came close to losing me to an ugly death and if it had not been for their faith in a new God, my journey would have been quite different. As we continued to practice living this new life for God, little did we realize this would become my life's journey? It did not take long for me to fall in love with the teachings of Jesus. The more I read the more I loved what I read. As I moved from a teenager to an adult, I made a very strong and determined decision this is how I would live my life.

I determined to continue to do everything right and pleasing to my God for as long as I lived. I decided to read God's word and pray daily to Him. I was determined not to let anything stand in my way or hinder me from my walk with Him. I soon realized should I make a mistake; He would take care of me. From then I decided this is my journey. This was who God made me to be, and I knew He would walk with me my entire life on earth and forever more. It's a wonderful, secure feeling!

My New Walk with God

"As ye have therefore received. Christ Jesus the lord so walk ye in him." Colossians 2: 6.

I knew I wanted to walk this journey depending on God to bring me through any struggles I might face. As a young woman

I determined to rely on His word to be my tower of strength. He let me know I was not alone on this life journey. I knew in my heart this was not going to be easy, yet I was determined to do things God's way. All I wanted to do was attend church. When I'm in church, the singing was always so touching and so comforting. The people were happy. The preaching was a new thing for me I could not understand everything I heard, just hearing brought me joy. I'm now in a new world.

The minister preached the word from the Bible and I learned how to understand what I read. I learned the songs that were sung during the services. In the months that followed, I made a definite decision to accept Jesus into my life. I was baptized. I wanted to live as a Christian. It was a big challenge for me. I wanted to do the right thing. I felt I owed my life to this God. Life meant everything to me now. I wanted to live a good, healthy life and wake up happy and enjoy each day as it comes. I did not want to be fearful of something bad ever happening to me again. Being with my family was something very special to me in every way. To be alive was a miracle of happiness that most people really could not understand.

As the months went by, we joyfully attended every church worship service as a family. We were learning a whole new way of living. We began to pray more and depend on God for all our needs. We learned God can provide for us and take care of us. Healing had become a way of life for us. We trusted in this truth as we began to share this with everyone we came in contact with. Even if we were criticized by relatives, we never stopped. We were experiencing the power of a real God. We realized how serious it was to get to know more about the true God. After going through such a horrible experience of brokenness, tears, sorrow, and coming so close to death, no one wanted to have to experience this ever again. We knew the best thing for us is to be faithful and serve God without hesitation.

I learned so much in such a short amount of time. I loved every moment. I read my Bible daily and even memorize the scriptures that I loved. This is to be my life's journey, and I vowed to travel all the way to the end even when it got rough along the way. I had my mind set and nothing will stop me, nothing.

Eventually the day came when the minister ask if I would share my testimony of what God had done for me. He wanted me to share about this miracle everyone was talking so much about and how I was delivered, set free, and saved from death.

Without thinking twice, I said, "Yes."

He was happy and said he would like me to do this in a few weeks. Then it dawned on me. I had to be ready to speak before all the hundreds of people attending church. This would be the first time I would be speaking before a large group of people, most of whom knew me while I was possessed.

I was not sure what I would say. These people had spent long hours, days and nights praying for me, and now the time had come for me to stand before them as a living testimony of the miracle of new life in Christ they had prayed for. I had to be brave. All I could think of was what to say and how to adequately express what I was feeling. How am I going to bring out the words that choked up in me? I was so nervous that my emotions were not allowing me to think right. I had so much to say, and yet I did not know how I'm going to present myself in front a church full of people. I had to build my self-confidence to be able to do this. I only had a few weeks to prepare my testimony.

Everything about my life was all so new to me. So much was happening so fast. The love and warmth and all the attention I was getting was unbelievable. I had gotten a lot of attention when they were praying for me. Now I was getting even more attention because of my new life. This was very overwhelming. I was a name on everyone's lips in their prayers, in their homes, and now all around me. Everywhere I went; my name would be mentioned and rejoiced over. This was an amazing experience for me.

I decided to talk this over with my family and ask them to help me to prepare. They told me as much as they could about what we had all been through, holding back some of the frightful stuff for fear we would have to go through again. So with that I prepared for the big day. I did quite a lot of praying and wrote down how I felt. I began to express my thoughts and feelings as I felt led to do and to be thankful to the God who made me whole and gave me a new life. This was all I could do at the moment. With the help and encouragement of the Christian people in the church, I felt I was ready to do this. I was determined not to let anything stop me. This was who I'm now and felt I would be for the rest of my living days. This was the journey Karma was meant to take. I needed to go forward without letting setbacks and criticism stand in my way.

Finally, the day came when I had to face this challenge to speak. This was my big chance to show the world what God

Karma

can do and share what He did for me. It was a very bright Sunday morning, different from all my other Sundays. I got up very early, read my Holy Bible, and I prayed the new way I learned to pray. I wanted to be ready spiritually. We all got dressed and left for the church. I had chosen a white satin and lace dress my grandmother had made for me. I chose white as a symbol of peace and purity which was how I felt about myself.

My family was all happy for me and encouraged me I could do this. I wanted to shine be beautiful. I wanted to be special. To look my best for my God. I felt very nervous on the drive to the church, but deep in my heart I knew God would make me brave and give me the strength to speak to this large crowd. We were greeted at the church with lots of handshakes and love. These people had great confidence in me. I began to feel tense; it's too late to back out now.

The time came for me to go up on the platform. I was anxious for this to be over. Everyone gathered around for prayer the adult choir begin to sing. The congregation began to worship which lasted about an hour. The minister took his place behind the pulpit and spoke from the Bible. He then introduced me. As my name was mention, my heart sank inside me. I encouraged myself saying, "I have to go on. These people prayed for my life. Now I stand before them alive and a new person. I need to give back to them."

I was experiencing a mixture of emotions about this whole thing, wondering if I could really do this. I was so tense, I lost my voice. I was a bit shy as I faced this crowd and so nervous my hands were shaking. The minister kept on talking about all that had happen to me from the day I was brought to the church to the day I was delivered. He gave a brief history of my life and the pain our family went through for me. Then he shared about how God had miraculously delivered me, changed me, and gave me a new life for all to see. Every word he spoke sounded so good.

How am I to add to what he just said? My heart was pounding even faster. I was sweating nervously again. For some reason I kept telling myself I do not know if I can do this. The thought would not leave me. Finally it came to my mind this was fear trying to hold me captive. I was struggling with myself. I began to change the way I was speaking to myself. I knew had to do this. Then I looked over at all the people sitting there waiting to hear what I had to say that morning. As I looked at my family, I felt an instant joy come over me. It was a very, happy feeling.

The minister finished speaking and all I heard was, "Now Karma will share her testimony."

With boldness I stepped forward to the pulpit and took the microphone as the minister handed it to me.

He looked at me and said, "You can do this."

"Yes," I responded and at that moment my hands stop shaking.

I stopped feeling nervous. All I felt was peace and joy within me. I was ready to do this and began to speak with a power I did not know I had. I spoke what was in my heart.

"I thank God for Jesus Christ and His love for me, for saving my life, delivering me from demon possession, setting me free, healed my broken body, for making me a whole human being, and giving to me a new life in Jesus Christ. I thank Him for my family who stayed with me, for my faithful parents, for all their sacrifices, the courage they had to believe in God for my life, and for not giving up on me and letting me die. They are everything to me. I thank God for my grandmother for the tremendous efforts she made to convince my father to try the church as a last resort. I thank God for her, and the people who stood with my family, and prayed with them for me that I would live. Thanks to this church and the ministers for their great faith in God and for standing with my family even when they were weak in their faith. I am thankful for so much love and friendship from everyone here. I am very thankful for the life Jesus has given me. He has made me a beautiful person. I owe my life to Him who made me who I am and what I will become in the future. Today, I promise I will live my life for Him. As long as I live, I am a living testimony of what Jesus can do. This day is the beginning of a new walk for me my life is in God's hands. I will continue to trust in Him to help me to live, have faith in Him, and depend on His strength to lead me through this life that I now have in Him. Thank you all so very much, Amen.

> *"In this was manifested the love of God towards us, because that God sent His only begotten Son into the world, that we might love through Him" I John 4:9.*

I spoke with a bravery I never knew I had, with tears running down my cheeks, and with a joy I never had before. After I was finished speaking, the entire church stood up and clapped and shouted praises to God on my behalf. What a tremendous moment of gladness and praises after praises. Then the minister walked toward me and laid his hands on me and blessed me. It was amazing! I'm now the girl with a tremendous testimony. Everyone was so proud of me and how far I had come in my new life. This was a new beginning for me and everyone who knew me my parents was happy for my decision to live the Christian life.

For God so Loved the World...

I continue to share my testimony everywhere I'm given an opportunity. Today, I'm still living my life for God in all that I do and will continue to do. Wherever my journey takes me. That first time was a day of victory for everyone who had a part in my deliverance and meeting God. It was a day of great rejoicing. A day I will always remember for the rest of my life. What a very blessed day it was! I felt God's love so real to me it was as if He was standing there with me. The presence of God was so powerful to me on this special day. It is not easy to explain what I was feeling. I had read about the love of God so many times. I feel that John 3:16 expresses His love so clearly.

> *"For God so loved the world that he gave his only begotten son that whosoever believeth in him shall not perish but have everlasting life." John 3:16*

Just to have been loved by the one true God, even before I knew Him, but who knew me and loved me for who I was and even the way I was is so amazing to me. He knew all that was within me and everything about my life. He knows and feels the same way about you. This is love at its greatest! This God is the one who can gave you life on earth and also promises life after death. This love you cannot and must not resist. It is a love you can share with others. There is no other love like it.

This is my experience of God's amazing love for me. No one could ever love me like He does. His love is forever and ever. I'm so happy that I'm able to share God's amazing love for me with others, and to thank Him and all those who had helped my family and me through the turmoil of my demon possession. I knew it was time to start living my new life the way God wanted me to live. There were many people greeting me with love and encouragement after I spoke. Many prayed for me showing me they really cared what The Lord did for me. I did not know how to respond to all this attention. I just felt it was God's way of showing me His love through His people. I had never felt so special before. It was a wonderful day and one I will never forget!

Chapter 5
GOD MAKES A WAY

"Jesus saith unto him I'm the way, the truth, and the life no man cometh unto the father, but by me." John 14:6

In learning to walk with Jesus. The new Karma started to live a bright new life of love joy and peace like I had never had growing up. All I wanted to do was keep on reading the Bible, and praying, and oh how I loved to sing songs about God. The words were so powerful and I felt so much love when I sang. A secret presence surrounded me and I said to myself, *I have an angel with me*. I could not explain it. All I knew was everything was right for me and I was happy. This was now my life and I was going to live a life of faith, sharing God's love for me and His saving power wherever my journey took me. I wanted everyone to know how very powerful God is, and. He can do anything we ask Him to do if we truly believe and trust in Him truly he is the way to new life.

My family and I committed to worship at this church regularly and learned to love the people. My parents dedicated their lives to the Lord and joined the church. I decided to join the youth choir because I loved to sing and wanted to keep on singing for my new found God. I attended Sunday school and youth group meetings, hungry for more Bible knowledge. Every time I went there was something new and exciting to learn, and I was growing as a new Christian. The Bible stories were so inspiring and helped me go the right way in my walk. I was willing to read, study, and learn how to correctly take my journey so nothing would hold me back. I began to soon learn about the struggles I would face as I continued my journey. MY only choice was to learn how to be strong and rely on God. Somehow I know this was not going to be an easy road.

The Young Man in the Blue Shirt

One Sunday morning we were singing, clapping, shouting praises to God, and just enjoying morning worship. The minister introduced a group of four handsome young men to sing specials songs for our congregation. As they were singing, my eyes fell upon one of the young men. As he sang his voice captured me and my heart was full of a sudden happiness. I had never seen anyone like him. He was tall and slender, dressed in a sky blue shirt and a nice black suit with a white tie. He was handsome he stood out to me his voice was all I could hear. I felt as if he was singing just for me. I could not keep my eyes off him. After the group finished singing, my eyes followed him to see where he sat. I was very curious to see if he sat with a girl. He sat down with a group of young people. I could not tell

God Makes a Way

if he had a girlfriend or not. I lost interest in the message the minister was preaching. I kept gazing over to where this young man was seated and could not concentrate on anything else. I was caught up in this young man in the blue shirt who did not even know I was staring at him.

When church was over and people started to greet each other, I watched as the group of young people disbursed. I was interested in seeing if one of the young girls belonged to him. I soon realized he was alone as everyone went their separate ways. After a while he looked across to where we were standing, walked over, and greeted our family. I knew then he was single for sure. I felt so happy when we left for home. I could not get him out of my mind. Eventually I mentioned to my sister about the singer in the blue shirt and told her I thought I liked him but did not know his name. This was strange for us as we were never allowed to talk to boys, and here I was telling her I liked the singer guy. All I knew was that I felt love for the first time in my life.

Every Sunday I looked for him at Church. I never talked to him and was embarrassed to ask anyone about him since I did not even know his name. I just waited and hoped he would see me and come over to talk to me. I don't know if he even noticed me. He seemed very popular with all the young people. He joined the youth choir and was there at the youth group meetings, too. It seemed like he never missed anything that was going on in the church. He kept singing in the church with the group. I liked seeing him every Sunday. I could not seem to help myself. Whenever I saw him I would be so captivated by him I could not concentrate on anything else. It was crazy! This went on for months. Only my sister knew how I was feeling. I could not share this with anyone else. I kept wishing I knew his name.

Then suddenly a strange thing happened. I came to church a couple times and did not see him. This went on for weeks and I wondered what had happened to him. Where did he go? I got very sad and wondered if I would ever see him again. Every time we went to church I looked for him hoping to see him again, but he was not there. I did not know who to ask about him and it bothered me that I did not even know his name. It was a mystery to me and I grieved for the next few months. I began to lose hope of ever seeing him again. My heart was empty.

Why was I feeling this way, I barely knew this person? I had never been in love and did not know what it felt like! This must be love, I thought to myself. I grieved he did not even know I was interested in him or how I felt. I wondered if I would ever be able to get over him, he was gone and there was nothing I could do. All I had to remember him was his blue shirt and his very captivating voice. I knew that memory would never leave me. I kept hoping that some day he would return. I purposed to not lose hope. I was not going to give up hope.

We continued to be in church as a family. This was very important to us. I got actively involved in the children and women's ministries. I wanted to share the love of God in my life with everyone to be a witness for Him. My siblings and I enjoyed the youth meetings and tried not to miss out on any. This gave us a chance to meet other young people like us. We were growing in the faith and loving what we learned about God.

Praying for My Future

"Trust in the lord with all thine heart: and learn not unto thine own understanding. In all thy ways acknowledge him and he shall direct thy path." Proverbs 3:5-6.

As I approached my seventeenth birthday, time was getting close when my parents would start talking about my marriage to my so called suitor. I was afraid I was destined to marry this man. All I could do was start praying for God to save me from all their plans and the guy my dad had arranged for me to marry. I did not want this to happen I started asking God for a Christian husband who would love me for who I am, take care of me, and was dedicated to serving God the way I wanted. I prayed for a husband who would attend church with me, and love the things that I loved like singing and reading the Bible. I poured my heart out to God asking for a Christian man who loved God and would want to attend church every Sunday and be proud to have me at his side. I just wanted to be loved all through my life. I was very specific in my prayers. I stated that the man I desired for a husband must be a dedicated Christian, have a desire to be involved in the ministry, be in Bible school, and want to preach, sing, and helping others that are in need in the church.

I desperately wanted to be rescued from the death sentence marriage to this other man. As I waited for God to answer my plea for a special husband, I began to check out the other guys in church. There were a few guys I thought might be the one God would want me to marry someday. However, this did not feel right talking to them. I soon realized I don't feel the same way I felt when I thought about the singer in the blue shirt. Even though we had not gotten to know each other, he was always in my heart. A stranger I did not know had already won my heart. I finally made up my mind to stop looking for the right guy and just keep my thoughts on the Lord. I concentrated on getting closer to God and letting His word be my guide. I was learning the process of having faith in God for something I needed. Hoping my stranger would come back into my life. I began to read every scripture on faith.

My decision now is to begin to live a life of faith and commitment fully serving God even if I never got a Christian husband. No matter what, ever happens I would never give up on my Lord. I wanted to live my life to please my Lord. Almost as soon as I settled this in my heart, I started to face some struggles with my parents. They could not understand why I wanted to spend all my life in the church. It was hard to explain to them what was in my heart, my desire for God, and my thoughts for my future. The battle really started when I told them I refused to get married.

The Spiritual Battle for My Family

"The thief cometh not. But for to steal .and to kill, and to destroy, I'm comes that they might have life and that they might have it more abundantly." John 10:10.

Things had been going great for us since we had become active Christians. My dad's fish business had started to prosper. My mom was happier than she had ever been and things looked good between them. My dad had even become an usher in the church. When I told my parents I did not want to get married, my dad tried to stop us from attending so many church meetings. He completely stopped attending. I could not believe he would turn away after all that God had done for us, the dynamic life changing experience, and all the blessings we had all received. What is all this about? I did not realize the devil was trying to steal the love of God from our family.

For his own selfish reasons, my dad was ready to give up his new life and return to his former ways. This was a great disappointment to us. We could not believe what was happening. What he was doing really bothered me, but we could not question him. His behavior hurt me more than anything. Every once in a while I would convince him to come to church with us, he would but not often. As I prayed I realized I needed to fight a spiritual battle for my family. I could not let this happen. They had stood for me when I could not stand for myself, now it was my turn to be strong for them.

My siblings and I remained in the church despite how my dad felt. We pressed on through the struggles and the hardships together. We loved the church and did not want to leave. It was a place of peace and happiness this was comfort for us. Though we were very young, we wanted to do the right thing. This was not easy for any of us as we struggled to learn this new lifestyle of serving God. Through it all God gave us an inner strength the courage to endure and be strong and stay close to each other. We decided to not gave up we trusted in God for answers.

Then one Friday evening we attended youth meeting, and saw my stranger was back. My heart was full with joy. I was so happy to see him talking and laughing with all the other young people. I could not believe my eyes. All I could think of is that he is back. I did not know for how long or what to say or how to act. I turned to my sister and told her the singer was back. We sat in the last row of pews in the church so we could leave as soon as the meeting was over as we always did. However, as the service began, the minister asked all of the people in the back pews to move to the front pews so we could be close to the rest of the youth. We move up to the front pews as requested and sat in the second row of pews.

Soon the singing was over its greeting time and we begin to greet everyone around us. As I turned around to my surprise I was right next to the singer. He greeted me with a soft hand shake. We looked at each other and smile at that instant I knew he was the one I would marry. This was the husband I had prayed for and God brought him back for me. The same feelings I felt the first time I saw him resurfaced. It was so real! I was anxious to know his name. I was determined to ask him, but had to wait until after the meeting. We smile at each other every time our eyes met. It was a wonderful feeling to see him after so long. This was love and in my heart I knew God had prepared him for me.

Then finally the meeting was over. Afterwards, we talked for a little time he told me his name. And I learned he had gone to do mission's work on an Island called Grenada. He said they were building a church there and he was part of the mission's team. As we said good-bye, he asked if I would be in church on Sunday and I assured him we would. As we left for home, I realized I did not know anything about missions work or stuff like that. I was still so happy and told my sister I had talked with him and really liked him. She knew I was happy, and kept this to her-self. She wanted me to be happy, but knew as well as I did how our dad would react. When he finds out.

I've been singing in the youth choir and now that he was back I got to see him every time we had choir rehearsal. We eventually started to talk more and more. I was slowly learning more about him and his involvement in various ministries. His focus was on missions and he was already in Bible school studying to be a minister. He was a Sunday school teacher, and very active in the church. This was exactly what I had asked God for in a husband! We began to spend a lot of time talking and getting to know more about each other. Our conversations centered on what we would like to do for the Lord. We both had a desire for the ministry and wanted to be good servants for the Lord! I mentioned to him how much serving the Lord meant to me and how I did not want anything or anyone to stop me. I told him how grateful I was to God for my new life and. I wanted to live only for him that's how it was going to be for me. He looked at me and spoke those same words right back to me. We were both very serious about our walk with the Lord, and I knew then God was bringing us together.

I did not tell him that I had prayed for him to come back or I had prayed for a Christian husband. We continued to talk about our lives and our dreams for the future without realizing how much we had in common. It did not take long before we fell in love with each other. I knew he was attracted to me by the way he looked at me. I was just waiting for him to express his love for me. Then I wrote him a very short love letter expressing my love for him hoping he would respond back to me. he did . His response was what I had been hoping and praying for. It made me so happy knowing he loved me and was serious about our relationship. We continued to write love letters to each other. It was our way of expressing our love since we were not allowed to go out on dates.

Within a few months he asked me to marry him. I was happy, but surprised. I never told him that my father had promised me to someone else. This was not easy for me to tell him. Finally I did and I explained how I felt about the other man and that it was not my choice. I told him how unhappy I was about the whole arrangement and I had tried to get out of it. There seemed to be nothing I could do at the moment. I saw the disappointment in his face when I finished telling him, I had to be honest with him. I told him I have been praying and did not know what to do. I was so afraid after I told him all this that it would be the end for us.

After a couple weeks had passed, he told me he was going to talk to my parents and ask for my hand in marriage. I was so happy to hear him say those words; I had to talk to my mom and my grandmother. They would have to talk to my father first on my behalf I was hoping with all my faith. I had, they would be on my side and stand up for me. They both knew my feelings towards this suitor. I knew my dad would be really mad at me if I did not go through with his choice of a husband for me.

I begin to panic, fearing what might happen so once again I started to pray. It seemed to be the only thing I could do to save myself from my dad's anger and get him to agree to allow me to marry someone else. I got brave and made a definite decision to tell my mom and grandmother. I needed their approval and they gave it to me. Everyone was happy for me, but my mom was worried about how to talk to my father about this guy I planned to marry. We both knew he would be very angry with me, her, and everyone in the house. I said to her I was ready to face the circumstances that would follow.

However one day she got the courage to tell my father. I had met a young man in the church and I liked him, and wanted to marry him instead of the one he had promised me to. My father flew off into a rage and told her he was not letting me have my own way. He was so mad he could not control the ugly things he was saying to her about me, and this guy I wanted to marry, and the church. It took him a few weeks to settle down, and then he asked me if I wanted to be married to the new guy in the church. Though I was very fearful, I said, "Yes."

My grandmother was there and she pleaded with him to let me marry the one I liked, pointing out I would be happy with the one I had chosen and not with the one he had chosen for me. He already knew how I felt about the arrangement he had made. I knew I was disappointing him and messing up his dowry plans. I knew I had to keep on praying for God to help me and to make a way for my father to stop his anger towards me. My mom and my grandmother kept trying to make him see things in a different way. I was really hurting inside.

My heart was crying within me because I felt I had brought sorrow on my family again. After all the joy we had experienced together, things were being disrupted because I had met someone and fallen in love with him, not the person whom my dad had in mind for me. I never gave up praying because I knew God could change my dad's mind. I was depending on the Lord to intervene in this situation. I prayed all the time. I never told any of this to my boyfriend. I did not want him to know what I was going through, but he saw the change in me and kept on asking me what was wrong.

Finally, I told him my father would never let me marry him. He said he was going to talk to my father and tell him he wanted to marry me. I begged him not to talk to him. He would not listen to anything I said. He was serious about marrying me and nothing would stop him. When I realized he was not giving up on me, I told my parents he wanted to talk to them. To my surprise they agreed. Still concerned what would take place at this meeting; I invited him to dinner at our house one Saturday evening. After we had dinner, the conversation started between my dad and my Christian boyfriend. It got really heated and they got angry with each other. My father was trying everything he could to discourage my boyfriend from marrying me. He kept refusing to give his consent for us to be married. My boyfriend left and I wondered what would happen the next time we saw each other.

Though we did not speak much after that sad night, he kept reminding me he would marry me someday and encouraged me to trust in the Lord. He even gave me Bible verses to read to help me have more faith. I read the verses and kept my trust in God. I was encouraged since that meant he was also praying about us. As the days went by I kept wondering if God could give me a new life free from demon possession, why wouldn't He do anything about this situation? I decided to forget about marriage and focus on God. God knew what He was doing, and only He would bring this to pass in my life. I knew it would take a miracle to make this happen for me, so I waited in prayer for God to work this miracle.

Time for another Miracle

"The name of the lord is a strong tower: The righteous run into it and are safe." Proverbs 18:10.

A few months passed and I found out my dad had talked to some people asking for advice on what to do about me. To his surprise every one of them told him to allow me to marry the man I liked. They told him since we both were in the same church; it would be good for us. He eventually agreed soon he had to return the portion of money he had gotten as a dowry for me. The family was very upset with him and told him he needed to stop me from doing this. My dad told them he could not stop this from happening. It created a big conflict between the two families, and we never saw them again.

After a couple months my father gave us his permission to be married. I thanked God for answering our prayers. He had made a way for us where there seemed to be no way! We were married in a small ceremony. We were very happy God had brought us together! Our married life would consist of church ministry which I felt very happy to do. I loved my husband and my new life. My walk with my lord was very rich with the fullness of his blessings. I missed my family very much. I loved going home to visit every weekend to be with my younger siblings. We remained a very close family.

I was seventeen and he was nineteen. There was a lot for us to learn as we began our married life together. We grew together as we built our life around the word of God and depended on Him to see us through any circumstance we encountered on our journey. We lived for one another and began building our future together in God. We rented a little one bedroom apartment in another village. We enjoyed our time of getting to know and understand our lives of love and commitment in this thing called marriage. My husband made a living working on a printing press. The money was not much, but we were very content with what we had. Our needs were always met! We always depended on God to answer our prayers for whatever we needed. We continue to be in church and to follow the Lord.

We soon discovered we had the calling of the Lord on our lives to preach the gospel. We were to face difficult times and many battles in the ministry, but we stood together and learned from the very beginning to be dependent and trust in God for His guidance. We never gave up though we would face discouragement many times in our new life together. Sometimes it seemed the more we worked for God the more the trials came our way. There were lots for us to learn, but we always agreed with one mind, and learned to work out our difficult times together. Whatever we faced, we trusted in each other and in our God who had brought us together.

Chapter 6
FROM TRAGEDY TO TRIUMPH

"The blessings of the lord, it maketh rich. And he addeth no sorrow with it." Proverbs 10:22

As a young wife, I learned to be an encouragement to my husband. There were times he would be so disappointed with different kinds of situations, with people, the church, and with his job. When discouragement set in, he would be hard to live with and I did not want this in our marriage. At first he refuse to talk about things that were bothering him, somehow I always knew when things were not going the right way. I had seen what happens to people when they were always discouraged I did not want that for us. So I prayed God would show me things in the spirit and asked the Holy Spirit to reveal things to me so we could live in victory rather than defeat. I had seen people live in misery. I saw this with my own parents and close relatives and I purposed this was not for us. We are children of God we belong to him.

After my deliverance and becoming a Christian, I visited the doctor many times. One of the things he told my parents. I may never be able to bear children. He said if I did become pregnant, there was a good chance of miscarriage because my body would not be able to handle the pressure of carrying a child. This was not good news for me, it made me sad, and I kept these things to myself and The Lord. I knew if I asked God for a miracle, He would do a miracle for me again. As time went by I kept on praying and trusting The Lord. God was so good to us and we became pregnant and had our first baby. We were blessed with a little boy, our special baby. We became parents again and I gave birth to our second child, another special little boy. We loved them so much and they brought much joy to us.

Our Family Continues to Grow

Within a year and a half, I was pregnant with baby number three. The house we were living in was too small for our growing family. We knew we had to find a bigger place to live. My father had brought some land and offered us a place to build our own house. We accepted his offer and built a two bedroom house. It was small but we were very happy. My husband changed jobs and sometimes it was hard for us, however we were always able to make it through.

I had our third baby, our first daughter. She was a beauty to behold and truly a bundle of joy. Her birth was a life and death delivery as I almost died giving birth to her. The umbilical cord had wrapped around her neck, Thank God we brought her safely home. All of my children brought me joy. Shortly after her birth, my husband along with other ministers from the church, travelled to different parts of the country to start new churches. My husband a very active, young vibrant, preacher. He loved working for the Lord and enjoyed singing and preaching. I loved to hear him operate in his calling. He was very faithful in everything he did. He never let anything hinder him from doing the work of the Lord.

He was involved in so many ministries there were times I stayed at home with the kids. We went with him as often as we could. There were many struggles as we strove to do the work of the Lord. This is what we wanted no matter what the cost. I never gave up my walk with the Lord though the enemy was always ready to try and steal my life. Though he tried to throw bad stuff at me, God was with me all the time. The devil never wins and he never will because I knew my life belonged only to God. I always had faith in my God to take care of us. I never doubted His word even if things did not go my way. I will always believe in Him for my life and my future.

Nothing Is too Hard for the God I Serve

"I will bless the lord at all times: his praise shall continually be in my mouth: Psalms 34:1

Trying to continue in the church and taking care of a husband and three small children was a big responsibility for me. It seemed the closer I drew to the Lord the more the attacks I received from the devil. Sometimes they would come very subtle, sometimes very forcefully. Two years after my baby girl was born I became very ill and had to be hospitalized with a bad kidney disease. It was so bad I felt as if I would die. Medication and weekly doctor visits became tiring for me. My husband stayed home to care for me and the kids. My mom helped as well. This went on for many months. I knew I had to fight this with all my strength. I prayed with my husband and we asked our church friends to pray for me during this time.

I remained actively involved in women's ministry in the church and these women were dedicated prayer warriors. We met every Wednesday for prayer for the needs of]the pastor and the families in the church. These women were examples of what godly women should be. We loved each other and I learned a lot from them. We were like sisters in the Lord. I had attended a lot of women's conferences and prayer retreats with them and now I needed them to pray victory for me. Once again I stood believing for God to heal me and let me live. I read every verse in the Bible on healing, having faith in the word. I began to believe that I'm healed.

I read the stories in the Bible about all the healing Jesus performed while He was on earth. As I read these stories, I believed once again for my healing. It took a long time of waiting and trusting in the words of the Lord, after a few months I was completely healed. From then to now I have never had another kidney problem. God miraculously healed me. I'm a living testimony of more miracles of what God can do for anyone who believes. Nothing is too hard for the God I serve. My husband was happy to see another miracle in our lives. My kids were taught from their early years to believe God and His word. We take them to church with us continually. They loved attending church. This was something they always looked forward to. Our little family was a blessed one.

We were very consistent with teaching our kids to be obedient, respectful, and loving others, as they were growing strong in the Lord. What a joy to watch them grow up as we nurture them in the Lord. We read the Bible as a family every night and had a small devotion with them. We taught them how to pray. And believe God for answers. It's wonderful, to listen to them pray. I was a very happy person,

A few years later my husband and I decided to have another child. It took a couple of years and then I found I was pregnant with baby number four. This was a very healthy pregnancy. I was doing great and we were very excited for this new baby, another very precious gift from God. Everything was going our way.

My husband was now the pastor of a small country church. The people loved us very much and were very faithful in their attendance. We travelled forty-five miles every Sunday morning to have church with them. Every Wednesday morning I would be there for the women's pray meetings and then drive back again on Thursday night for our mid-week church service. This was our weekly schedule, Soon it began to get very hard for me being pregnant with three other children. The kids were getting older and were very happy about having a new baby in the house.

We were in full time ministry and committing all our time to the work of the Lord. Things were sometimes a little rough for us financially, but God never let us suffer for lack of anything. He always provided for us. At times it was in a big way and other times in a small way. Nevertheless He took care of us. We always had enough. We knew the call into full time ministry would not be an easy call; we obeyed and depended on God faithfulness to see us through.

From Joy to Sadness

"The eyes of the lord are upon the righteous. And his ears are open unto their cry." Psalms 34:15.

I gave birth to our second beautiful daughter on April 7th, but our precious little baby died two hours after her birth. I never understood the complications that lead to her death; I heard her cries after she was born, I was devastated after her death, and very angry with the doctors for not taking the right precautions to save her life. All I knew was everything was fine and I delivered a live baby. Not much explanation was given about what really happened or how she died. I may never know for sure, I felt it was carelessness on the part of the hospital staff. Apparently there was a shortage of nurses so I did not have the help. I needed during my daughter's birth. I held her so close to me just briefly and loved her!

Then a few hours later a nurse came and told me my baby girl had died. When I asked her what happened, she refused to tell me anything except they were calling it crib death. She would not say another word and just walked away leaving me crying for my baby. I did not know what crib death was, all I knew was my baby was dead. This was very hard for me to cope with. I begin to scream and shout they had killed my baby.

After shouting for a couple hours, I pleaded with them to let me see her. I was allowed to see her little body. The only memories I have, is of her little cries and her still little body.

I grieved deeply in my heart for her. I remained in the hospital a few days for observation. They were concerned that I was having a mental break down and kept me heavily sedated. They wanted to keep me quiet. Oh how I wished I had the power to bring her back. A few hours ago I was holding a crying newborn and now my baby was dead. My heart was full of emptiness. I felt as if part of me had died. I could not explain how I was feeling. All I could think of was how I'm to explain to our three children their baby sister was not coming home.

The doctors gave my husband their explanation of what went wrong. There was nothing we could do but go home and rely on each other for comfort and trust in God for my healing. During the months that followed, I kept on grieving for my baby. I did not want to talk to anyone or even go out the house. Our friends and relatives came to visit me I turn them away including my church friends. This was hard for them; I was so deeply embedded in sadness. I was not able to care for my other three small children. My husband had to work in church ministries and try to deal with my behavior. He was always very loving and caring and concerned over my health.

The doctors at the hospital advised us not to have any more kids. I had experienced too many complications during all my pregnancies. I needed to be very careful not to get pregnant again. This made me mad as if it was my fault my baby died. I felt it was their fault I lost my baby. They were the ones responsible and they were just covering up their mistakes. Of course, was their word against mine and I did not have all the facts about what went wrong. I did know the nurse attending me was in training and not sure what she was doing. During the delivery she called for the doctor, but help came too late as she did not have the training for what was taking place. I was kept heavily sedated as remain calm. At all times.

I try very hard to bring myself out of this sadness. I did my best to overcome the feelings. Finally, with much prayer from all my friends and all the encouragement from my husband and family, I began to feel better and stronger. However, inside me was a craving for a baby. These feelings just would not go away. I went to visit our family doctor to make sure I was getting better and my health was in good condition. He told me my blood count was very low and so was my blood pressure. He then told me try not to get pregnant because in my condition. I could die giving birth. It would be in my best interest not to have any more children.

This was not what I wanted to hear. I left his office very disappointed. How could this be? He could treat me with medicine. To make me well now he tells me what he thinks is best for me? In my anger I purposed in my heart to prove him wrong. Three months later I became pregnant with baby number five. When I went back to visit him and told him the good news I was pregnant, he was not very nice. He advises me not to have this baby, because it was too soon after my last pregnancy. I told him I was aware of all my health issues and felt I could handle this. I then told him he was wrong about me and this baby. I intended to prove this to him.

I made up my mind not to listen to his negative reports. And refuse to listen to what he was saying to me. I would do things to keep myself strong like eating healthy meals and getting plenty of rest and checkups. So I could carry this baby full term. I was depending on my God to give me good health and the strength I needed. I was warned about the dangers of having another baby and the risk I was taking with my life not only by the doctors, but by everyone in our family. I was a brave woman and a desperate mother. This was a test for me and I was determined to let my husband and my family knows I trusted my faith in God to carry me through.

When I told the news to my husband he was concerned for my life. I told him I knew the risks and that I had prayed and asked God for this child. I was trusting in God for this child. I had asked God for a girl and I was sure that God would take care of me and this baby no matter how terrible things might look for me. My husband looked at me in amazement and I saw the despair in his eyes. He did not want to lose me. I could only hope he would understand and sure enough he did. He sent for my mom so I will tell her my good news. When I did she was furious with me and reminded me what the doctor had said. I told her what I had told my husband. I ask her to give me her support and help me take care of our other three special kids. She was not happy with me and worried that something would go wrong and I would not be able to have this baby, but she was there for me.

I was very confident that everything would be fine for me. I've proved the power of God in my life time and time again. I'd learned the scriptures and how to live believing in them.

Living a life for God was vitally important to me. I faced many trials during this pregnancy and there were a lot of obstacles along the way. Though the months ahead were very trying and my body wanted to give up on me, deep in my heart my belief in God lived on. I knew that everything would be fine for me and my baby, I was not going to let anything deter me from receiving this gift from God. I must admit there were days I wondered if I had made the right decision for my life. Doubt tried to creep in and I would ask myself what I would do if something went wrong? Then I was reminded of something I read in the Bible that lifted my spirit. Jesus had promised He would never leave me or forsake me. He said He was always with me until the end. I held onto that promise.

During this pregnancy, we were asked to travel fifty miles to another church where my husband became an associate pastor. We loved the people there and they loved our family. The drive was very long and tiring with our three children, but we continued to be faithful. I was always at his side and ready to be an encouragement to him. He knew he could always depend on me to cheer him on. It was not hard. He was a powerful preacher a great man of God he loved the word. He lived by them every day. We never questioned the Lord when we had rough times, instead we trusted in Him to bring us through any trials. We experienced many battles, but we knew that God had been faithful to us and would be until the end! We knew we had to fight for our victory.

I was eight months along in my pregnancy when I went into labor. I could not believe this was really happening to me. It was Sunday night and my husband had gone to preach at a church meeting. I had stayed home with the kids. My parents lived next door, but I could not call them. By this time they would have been asleep and would not have heard me. I did not want to leave my three kids alone asleep. I was afraid if I went to wake my parents I might not be able to come back to my home. And get into the house. The only thing left for me to do was pray that my husband would come home soon so he could take me to the hospital.

I prayed and prayed and finally he got home. He ran and got my parents to stay with the kids, then rushed me to the hospital. I knew I was going to give birth soon. When we arrived at the local hospital, the nurse on duty examined me and told us she could not deliver this baby. They did not have the equipment or staff to deliver a breach birth at eight months. They told my husband he would have to drive me to the big hospital as there was no ambulance available there either. My husband loaded me back into the car and went speeding, running every stop light, hoping to get me there before the baby came. We did not want to lose this baby! Our faith was fully activated as we believed God cared very much what happen to us and our baby.

We arrived at the hospital around midnight and were attended to immediately. Through it all, I trusted God for this baby to live. When the doctor examined me, he began to explain the complication of a breach eighth-month premature baby, this he said was a life and death situation. As he talked about all the complications and what could go wrong, I reached over, grabbed his hands, and pleaded with him to do everything he could so my baby would live.

He looked at me and replied, "It is a fifty-fifty chance, I will do everything I can to help your child live."

I cried out with all my strength, "God, please save me and make my child live."

It was a miracle when at 1:20 a.m. I gave birth to a lovely baby girl. In our country dads were not allowed in the birthing rooms. I was alone with the doctors and nurses and my faith in God. I must say I held on to my faith in God. The joy of having another baby girl was overwhelming. With tears streaming down my face, I asked the doctors if my baby would be alright. He said our baby had to remain in the incubator as she was having problem breathing. I cried and cried upon hearing those words. A midwife who was assisting the nurses told me she had delivered many babies, but never had a breach delivery like this one. This was a very difficult delivery especially at the eighth months of pregnancy. I asked her again if my baby would live.

She looked at me and said, "Your faith in God will make her live. You will not lose her."

Words of comfort fill my heart. After she finished caring for me, she left and I never saw her again to thank her. She was my angel sent to help and encourage me. I was given a sedative to help relax me. As I was getting anxious to know how my baby girl was doing. I eventually fell asleep and was awaken at about three in the morning by another nurse holding our baby girl.

"Do you want to see your baby? She is alive," the nurse asked with a smile. I was so tired from the trauma, of the delivery I quickly said a big happy, "Yes!"

As I held my precious little miracle girl, I was so overjoyed and my heart was pounding with thanksgiving to God for giving me the little girl I had asked for. I had told everyone I was having this baby by faith, and now I'm holding her in my arms. God made it possible for her to be here with us!

She needed much medical care. I remain in the hospital eight more days. This was a time for me to rest and allow my body to start the healing process. My husband came to visit us at the hospital with our three children. What a joy it was for them to see me and meet their new baby sister. Truly the joy of the lord is my strength. Our family is now complete with two boys and two girls. It was a wonderful feeling. My husband and I were so happy! I knew I would not be having any more kids. This little blessing was our last. I'm now to devote my time to raising them the way the Lord would have us do. As young parents, we learned parenting skills the hard way and enjoyed every moment of our children's lives as they grew up. What wonderful blessings God gave us in each of our children!

Chapter 7

NOTHING IS IMPOSSIBLE FOR OUR GOD

"But Jesus beheld them, and said unto them. With men this is impossible: but with God all things are possible." Matthew 19:26.

My little girl was fully able to breathe on her own and feed after eight days. The doctors were amazed at all that happened. My faith to believe, that my baby and I would live. Touched them we left the hospital together and I rode home a very happy mother. As we drove our new daughter home that happy day, the Spirit of God spoke to my husband and said to him, "You will raise this baby in the USA." At the time we knew that was not possible for us. We were not even thinking of leaving our home. Our children, the ministry, our church, and most of all the people we grew to love we lived our whole lives in Trinidad. How could this be what was God saying to us?

In our hearts we always knew that the Lord had His hands on our lives. We had always been obedient to His call and the leading of the Holy Spirit. We could not figure out what this meant or how this will come true. One thing we knew for sure, the Lord never made mistakes. We arrived home amidst all the excitement of a new born baby and the joys of our other three children seeing their little sister come home. I was so happy I just began to praise the Lord for my life, our new baby, all our children, and all He done in our life. I was so very grateful to be home with my family and to look forward to a long happy life.

My husband was in full agreement with my decision to not have any more kids. We were not going to take another risk. I could enjoy motherhood and care for my little blessings. I knew how much they needed me and how important my presence was in our home with them all the time. We showered them with lots of love and taught them the right things in life as they all were growing up. We wanted the very best for them. We did not have a lot of money, but we were always happy.

A year after the birth of our miracle baby girl we made a big decision to pioneer a church where we were living. All the traveling had become too much for the kids and I. We knew we had to make some changes in our lives; my husband gave up the associate pastor positions in the other churches. We agreed that this small area where we lived could use a church and so, with the help of relatives and neighbors we did. This was wonderful as we did not have to travel many miles to church any more. Starting the church in the neighborhood changed our lives. We gained so much respect from the neighbors. These amazing people saw Christ in us and were a constant testimony of faith.

Three years after we started the church, we were faced with the worst attack in our lives. This was a very nice warm afternoon. Our kids were out in the front yard playing a ball game called Cricket which is played with a wooden bat and a ball. One person throws the ball toward the person with the bat, who hits the ball and then runs across the ground to touch the winning pole. This type of game is very popular in the West Indies and England and many other countries, it's a very fun game to play and also to watch. My husband loved to play this game and so did our children.

An Ever Present Help in Times of Trouble

"God is our refuge and strength, a very present help in trouble." Psalms 46:1.

On this warm afternoon, I was cooking dinner and my husband was resting after a long day of work. Suddenly we heard loud screams coming from our kids. We ran out the house to see what had happened to them. We could not believe our eyes! They were being attacked by killer bees! Our oldest son had hit the ball across the yard into a nearby open field. When they went to fetch the ball, the bees attacked them. All we could do was try to beat the bees off them as they ran into the house for shelter. My husband and the three kids ran into the house for safety. I did not run with them. I went looking for my baby. She did not know what was going on. I ran to her and grabbed her, placed her under my house dress, and started to run up the steps. The steps were covered with swarming bees fighting to get into the house. I did not know what to do. I started to run to my parent's home for safety as fast as I could. I was being attacked by the bees even as I tried to run. They were in my hair and my body was cover with them. It was an eerie feeling having bees crawling all over my body. They were stinging me as I fought to protect my baby girl. I began to feel faint and could not run anymore. Desperate to save my baby, I made it to the fence close to my parent's house, pushed her through .and shouted for her to run as fast as she could to mama's house. She was smart enough and ran as fast as she could call for mama, as I stood there watching to be sure she made it to safety.

As I turned to go back to our house, I ran right into a swarm of bees. My dad heard my little girl calling out, "Mama, Mama." He knew something was wrong the minute he saw her climbing up the steps to their house all by herself. He shouted to my mom saying something must have happened to Karma, Kenneth, and the children. He reached out and took our baby girl into the house. My mom held my baby as my dad ran out to try and save me from the killer bees. All he could do at that point was make a fire to smoke the bees away from on me. The neighbors watched in horror as they all thought that I would die. My husband and three kids were safe in our house had no idea what was going on with me. My husband was treating the other children thinking I had run to safety.

By this time I was getting weak and ready to blackout. My Dad was having a smoky fire going when suddenly my younger brother just happen to drove by to visit us. He saw me out in the yard jumping around like a crazy woman.

My parents shouted out, "There are killers bees attacking your sister!"

My brother ran as fast as he could, grabbed a bucket of water, and dump the water over me. Then he pushed me into his car and drove me over to the next door neighbor's house. After which he drove back to our house to check on my husband and the kids. My brother showed great courage on that frightful day. My brother and one of my cousins drove the kids to the hospital to be treated for the bee stings. My husband, covered in bee stings himself, drove me to the hospital. When we got there the doctors said there was not much they could do for us. They treated us for bee poisoning, but expected us to die from the stings we had all over our bodies. The medicine they gave us made us vomit. We were all admitted to the hospital for several days.

My husband kept repeating the words we shall live and not die over and over again. My brother and cousin stayed with us. They were very helpful answering questions for the doctors as we could barely say a word. Soon all the neighbors were there with us and so was our church family. They were all standing around praying for us. My husband recovered the next day and the kids were released within a couple days after. I remain one week in the hospital. They kept saying there was no hope for me. The medicine was not working; as it was given to me I vomit right back up. I could not keep anything in my stomach they gave up trying to give me any more medication. The doctors said it's no use it's only a matter of time.

I had a lot of itching and scratching from the bees stings over my body. It was very painful. They tried all they could to keep me alive. Finally I began to show signs of recovery. The doctors said it was a miracle. I was release from the hospital swollen from all the stings I had received. We were a mess and people expected us to die as no one had ever lived through one of these killer bee attacks. We were the talk of the village as our whole family lived under the fear of death.

By the mercies and grace of our God, we all lived to tell the frightful event. When the attack was reported to the health environment department, they came out to destroy the bees. They discovered there was a huge bee hive and told my husband they were millions of bees there which could have attacked the entire neighborhood. They said we were very lucky to be alive. They eventually destroyed the entire hives.

Today we can honestly say we defeated death. The people of the village were amazed to know we were alive after many of them had actually witnessed the attack of the killer bees. We can truly say God is a very present help in times of trouble. He saved us as a testimony of His love and grace in our lives so we could continue doing His work. We know without a shadow of a doubt that nothing is too difficult for our God to do for His children.

We came home after our encounter with the killer bees and life continued as normal for our family. My husband had a preach engagement schudule in a church on the Island of Barbados. We went and the meetings were marvelous. We shared what had happen to us and the people knew it was a miracle we had survived the killer bees. This was a big testimony for our family since anyone who got attacked by these bees generally died instantly! We continually give praise to our God for saving our lives.

A Living Example of God's Love and Grace

"And he said unto me my grace is sufficient for thee: For my strength is made perfect in weakness." 2 Corinthians 12:9.

In the years that followed, God blessed my husband with a very good job. The blessings began to flow and we were able to remodel our small house into a four bedroom. We were also able to purchase a nice car in great condition. We had a small church and felt it was time to expand the small building. Family and friends helped us build a nice church. We lived in a very poverty stricken area. We had the privilege of preaching the Gospel and saw many come to make a decision to serve God. This was not easy, but very fulfilling for us. A lot of them held fast to their old religious beliefs until something took place in their lives they would come to us for help. We were always ready to help them no matter how big a problem they had. We gained their respect and appreciation and learned how to adapt to the neighborhood we were living in.

The people liked having a church in the area and were happy to help when we decided to expand the building. Meanwhile, the Lord was blessing us in many ways. We wanted to share our blessing with others and went about helping the needy families in the area. We also took in young people who had no home and had them live with us. Our family loved doing these things for the Lord.

We did face some challenges along the way, but we never let them hold us back. There were struggles of all kinds and criticism from a few people who did not understand what we were doing and why we did what we did. We preached the gospel, believed in the Bible, and lived what we preached. We visited the sick and the poor. We became a friend to those that needed a friend. Soon I became a mother to many young people who needed someone in their lives for love and support, and encouragement or just needed someone to listen to them and loved them for who they are. God gave me a

Special gift of love for them all! We nurtured these people believing they were sent to us by the Lord. We reached out to them in every way possible, showing God's love for them.

Ministry is hard work. We lived, loved, and served the people of our community like a family. We prayed they would learn to depend on the Lord, trust in Him, and not look to be dependent on us. We did our best to show them the way to the Lord and how to have faith in God. We saw many miracles and witnessed many lives changed. We were blessed when we saw some of them desire the things of God and want to dedicate their lives to Him. This was our church family and no one except us knew the labor that went into the hard work. We had a Sunday school that blossomed with a lot of small kids. The women were very talented and used their talent to help one another in various ways. They learned from each other so did the men.

Nothing Is Impossible for Our God

We were growing in numbers by the grace of God as we brought them hope for a better life. They were genuine and very sincere about serving God and turning from their old life to living a new lifestyle of love for God. What we had was not a religion; it was a lifestyle of understanding who they were to God. They came because we made them feel important and loved. This was so very rewarding to us.

We continued to keep ministering wherever the Lord opened the door. As our church grew, we started to attend many church conferences and retreats to help us grow in areas where we were weak. I eventually got more involved in different women's ministries that enriched my own life and also helped me to minister to the many women God would allow me to minister. I always loved helping women in their walk with the Lord. I was very blessed to have Godly women in my life to learn from and to be an example to me. I then passed on what I learned to the women God placed in my life. This was very fulfilling for me. I found joy in what I did for others. I always felt .I could be an example to other women who had a desire to serve God. There's beauty in God's love and the love you share with his children's.

I believed He had called me to be a witness of His mighty love and grace. I prayed He would send me to the ones who needed Him the most. I'm always willing to share God's amazing love wherever He sent us. My husband and I begin to travel around the country starting small churches with the assistance of many other ministers. We also travelled to the Caribbean Islands to preach in crusades. This was very enriching in our lives. Wherever we went people needed to know about the real God and what He could do in their lives if they would let Him.

There were times of tiredness, but the Lord carried us through during those tough times. We reached out to our minister friends for encouragement and they would speak into our lives and refresh us! Without the support of other ministers and their churches, we could not have been successful. We needed them in our lives to help strengthen us and to pray for us. There were lots of discussions and planning to be done. Meeting with other minister's help. We were determined to stand strong knowing no battle could be won for the Lord if we gave up. No victories would be ours if we did not fight a good fight of faith. We refused to live in defeat and depended on the Lord for His guidance. We grew closer to Him and wiser in the ways of the Lord.

We discovered that our lives would be a journey of trials and testing. There would be time of happiness and sadness which will not always be easy! However we learned to endure the challenges that came our way. There were sacrifices we would have to make as we sought to fulfill the call God had placed on our lives. We were willing to do what it takes to accomplish what He had sent us to do. God was the center focus in our lives. Our children knew and were growing up to love the things of God. We taught them the ways of the Lord and to be obedient to His voice. We made our lives an example to them of how important it is to stay close to God. We had many opportunities to reach out to young people and children everywhere we went to preach the gospel. This brought us great joy as we watched our children serving the Lord right alongside us. We thanked God for what He's doing in their young lives.

We were a blessed family and we were givers in all we did for the Lord. We never asked anyone to fund our ministry. My husband worked a job and God always provided when there was a need. Our lives proved miracles take place when you have faith in the real God. In fact, we began to experience more and more miracles in our lives and in the lives of those in our congregation. We knew without a shadow of a doubt the word of God never fails when we put our trust in Him. Most of all prayer changes things we did just that as we continued our journey with Him!

A Heart for Other Ministers

The many years that followed one of our minister friends shared with my husband a vision he had for ministers to come together for a time of refreshing, fellowship, and holding each other up in prayer and encouragement. He believed every minister needed someone to strengthen them, to share their dreams and vision for their ministry, as well as a safe place to unburden themselves, and be free in their spirit to receive a fresh vision an anointing for their ministry from God.

As he spoke, my husband caught the vision and agreed to host such a meeting at our church with five other ministers. My husband suggested a prayer breakfast. It was a great meeting that first Saturday morning. From then on I enlisted the help of the other women in the church and we prepared the breakfast for these ministers. This was the beginning of many more prayer breakfast meetings to follow. They would meet every third Saturday morning at our church. This was such a blessing to them the number of attending ministers grew rapidly. The ministers had the freedom to reach out to each another. This was a very inspiring time for them. Ministers came from far and near. It did not matter where they came from they all had a need for this type of fellowship. The Lord moved upon their hearts and they were all blessed.

Months went by and they kept holding these meetings. It's just so amazing to watch a vision from a man of God come to pass, and to witness new ministry birthed that benefited so many other ministers. Our women who worked with me were very blessed to see God working in these ministers' lives and their ministries. As we prepared breakfast for them, we heard the men praising God and preaching to each other. The power of God was very rich amongst these ministers. We always looked forward to these meetings and were honored to host them in our church. Since then a ministers' fellowship has been established. There are hundreds of other ministers who have joined this fellowship which expanded throughout Trinidad, the Caribbean, South America, Canada, and the United States of America. It is now a well-established ministry fellowship.

At these meetings my husband grew very close to these men of God as they prayed for each other. They bonded together and they grew in grace, knowledge, and wisdom. I've learn to love and respect these men and held them in high esteem. They still have a special place in my heart.

A New Year. A New Call

Ye have not chosen me. But I have chosen you. and ordained you. "John 15:16"

A few years later, the Lord spoke to my husband at a midnight New Year's Eve service. I was leading the worship he was playing his guitar along with the other guitar player. The power of the Holy Spirit was so rich in the worship there was a powerful anointing on the congregation. While everyone, was engulfed in the worship. The Holy Spirit spoke to my husband and told him he was going to have to give up everything and go on the mission field. My husband was in total submission to the Holy Spirit of God.

The Holy Spirit then spoke the words of Jesus to my husband, "Do you love me more than these?" When my husband responded, "Yes," the Holy Spirit said, "Then give this up and come follow me."

This happened three times that night during the worship service. My husband felt this was in reference to the church, the people, and everything that we had accomplished in the ministry. No one knew what had happened to him that night, everyone felt a very strong anointing during the worship. Many said it was the best it had ever been. We had a great service that night and the people overflowed with joy and praises to God. This was very amazing! I was extremely happy to see the congregation in worship to God in their own way, and to know they had such liberty in the presence of our great God. As their tears flowed, I could tell they had experience the touch of the Holy Spirit. This was a very blessed night!

When the service was over we usually host an after midnight party to celebrate the New Year. Everyone and their families stayed over in the church and we celebrated until dawn. We had lots of food and drinks and games. This was a fun night for all. I observed my husband was not talking much. I asked him if he was alright. He said yes I knew he was bother about something. I also knew he would tell me what was on his mind when the time was right. Somehow I felt he had received from the lord I just waited for him to tell me.

A few days went by and he finally told me about his experience New Year's Eve night. He said God spoke to him to give up all and go on the mission fields. I was not ready to hear what he had to say. I did not doubt he had heard from the Lord, it's what the Lord told him made me want to go into prayer. I knew this was a very big decision for us to make. I was not ready for such a change. Everything was going great. Why should we have to leave?

This would not be easy for us, but I told him, "You have to do what God called you to do."

We kept this to ourselves for about two years until one Wednesday morning our senior pastor came home from a trip to the United States and stopped to visit with us. He told my husband he had a word from the Lord for us. He said to my husband the Lord had spoken to him about us going to the mission field. As he was speaking he was confirming what the Holy Spirit had spoken to my husband two years before at the New Year's Eve service. Then our pastor mentioned he had

Nothing Is Impossible for Our God

met a minister at a minister's conference in Texas who needed a full time minister to take over an organization and overseer a couple of churches in Belize. Our pastor told them about my husband. He had confidence my husband would be the person for such a work and would be willing to make the sacrifices to get the job done.

My husband agreed to take the position and move to Belize. We began to fast and pray about this. We wanted God's will and the leading of the Holy Spirit. In a few months things changed the ministry we were expecting my husband to oversee was handed over to another Pentecostal organization. We knew the Lord had other plans for us. However my husband knew somehow we would be leaving our church and the people we had grown to love so much. This bothered me my heart was sad. I knew we were doing a good work here. I did not want to leave. Then one Saturday morning my husband shared with the ministers in the fellowship that he felt the call to the mission field. They prayed with him and told him the Lord would lead him and spoke words of wisdom to him. Our senior pastor was a very good friend his advices to us was prayer and seek God's will and timing.

My husband and other ministers were invited to attend a minister's conference in Portland, Oregon. Our senior pastor encourages my husband he should attend and trust God for guidance as to where He wanted us to go. My husband and the other ministers made the trip to Oregon for the conference. And were bless as they received. Word from the Lord concerning the growth f their ministries. and the callings in their lives. They had a very refreshing time and met many ministers from different parts of the world and various other ministries. This was also a time for my husband to learn where God was leading us.

They all arrived home to their families and their churches with new dreams and new visions for their ministries. When my husband came home from the conference, he was so blessed. I knew he had received word from the Lord. I felt in my spirit that we would have to leave our church and the people we loved. I did not know how soon this would be and. I was not looking forward to this; somehow I knew it was coming. That previous year we had seen a lot of success in the ministry even though there had been some tough times along the way. We held on to the word of God and believed He would bring us out victoriously as He had done this in so many different ways.

We had always followed the call of God on our lives, but something was different with my husband this time when he came back from Oregon. I knew he's a man of the word and very dedicated to the ministry and the calling on his life. No matter where it led us or how hard it might be, I'm always ready and willing to do whatever we were called to do. I've read many times of people in the Bible giving up all to follow Jesus. They had given up houses, land, and families. These people had great faith in Jesus. I also learned if we put our hands to the plough and looked back, we were not fit for God's kingdom work. I felt in my heart I was ready to go all the way with Jesus. He knows everything about our future so I was determined to trust and follow Him. Even though I did not realize what I was doing, I was getting myself ready for something new.

Be a Sarah

Then finally one day my husband told me and our children what was in his heart. As prepared as I thought I was, I was not ready for what my husband said to us. He mentioned the Lord was calling us to the United States. To do this we would have to give up everything. I did not want to leave the church we had work so hard to build and everyone I loved. I did not know if I was ready for such a big change so I began to wrestle with the Lord in my spirit. I kept asking my husband over and over for the next week, how can this be? I knew the Lord had spoken to him, but I was wondering why God had not spoken to me. Had I been too busy and not listening to God? I made up my mind not to leave until God confirmed this to me. My husband told me when God called him he called me, too.

Day after day, night after night my husband tried to encourage me. I refused to pay any attention to what he had to say. In my heart I knew he was being obedient to the Lord, I was comfortable and very happy where we are serving the Lord. Why change now and go to a foreign country where we knew no one? How can this be happening to us? I became selfish in my own way and began to question God and seek an answer from Him for myself. Eventually, I mentioned to our women's prayer group what I was experiencing and what the Lord wanted for us. They began to pray for us so I would be submissive to the Holy Spirit.

I cannot explain why I was being so resistant other than to say I was enjoying the comfort and all the blessings in our life where we were, I did not want that to change. Weeks turned into months and my husband told our congregation what the

Lord had spoken to him. They were more receptive than I was. They were sad to hear that someday we would be leaving them. With constant prayer and much encouragement from our church family, I decided to fast and pray and wait on the Lord to confirm to me His plan. I finally surrendered, gave up my feelings, and waited for an answer from the Lord.

One sunny Monday morning at about ten o'clock while I was washing dishes, the Lord spoke to me saying, "Just be a Sarah and follow him with faith."

This was shocking to me. I dropped everything and began to read about Abraham and Sarah. I was in for a big surprise. On that very same day the Lord spoke to my husband and told him tell me be a Sarah. That evening my husband tried to talk to me again about leaving. I again refused to listen to him. Then he spoke the words God said to him and told me just be a Sarah. I immediately knew this is the answer. There could be no more resisting. I just looked at him and laughed. Before he could say another word to me I told him the Lord had spoken those same words to me that very morning. He was relieved he did not have to try to convince me anymore.

The effectual fervent prayer of a righteous man availeth much."James 5:16"

There was so much to do to prepare to leave the country. We had to go to the American consulate to retain traveling visas to come to America. My husband eventually shared with all the ministers in the fellowship we would be leaving and each one was sad but happy for him. His other friends, his employer, his co-workers, and all our relatives all reacted to the news. Some thought we were not doing the right thing. This was hard to explain to many of them the call of God on our lives. Serving God was one thing to them, but leaving for a foreign country was hard for them to understand.

We went to the American consulate and realized we would not be able to bring our two sons with us. This was the beginning of our faith being tested for this trip. We decided to leave them in the care of our relatives. Which was extremely difficult for us? We did this knowing God had a plan for us. Leaving everyone was a painful thing to do. The sadness was overwhelming for us. We were set to leave the country on May 25th. As the time drew near, we experienced the pains of saying good-bye to all those we loved.

Then my family was struck by tragedy. My dad passed away on my youngest daughter's sixth birthday. This was not easy for any of us especially with me leaving in a few months. The time of mourning was a time of deep sorrow for us, yet I knew I had to leave. My deepest concern was for my mom. This was the hardest on her with me leaving. She depended on me a lot. I knew she would miss us very much. We lived next door to each other, and my husband and I had been caring for her and my dad. With my dad gone she was already lonely and soon we be leaving for America, My other seven siblings would be there for her and the other grandchildren. I knew she would always have someone to be with her. I did my best to encourage her to hold on and promised her I would continue to take care of her even when I was away.

A Childhood Dream Comes True

Our church had a farewell party for us. The congregation was in tears as they expressed what we meant to them and how much they loved us. Seeing us having to leave, was a loss for them but they knew the Lord had plans for us. In the party my mom stood up and reminded everyone of a dream I had when I was a little girl. She said I had always dreamed of going to America. Every time I saw an air plane passing overhead or looked at a greeting card with snow and silver dust on it, I would tell everyone I am going overseas. This had been my dream as a little girl, I've grown up to think it was impossible for that dream to ever come true. I had eventually forgotten all about my dream. I thought it would never happen and now that dream was coming true. After she was done speaking, I started to laugh out loud. I remembered the many day dreams. I had done with my siblings.

This has been a very blessed farewell party. Each person shared a little of what was on their hearts and how much we meant to them. Many of them had been with us from the very beginning of our ministry. We had been part of their journey and they had been part of ours. I realized God had placed people in our lives to be a blessing to us, hold our hands, stand with us, pray, and cry with us. They encouraged us when we needed them and helped us to bear others burdens. They were there for us. There were some who just did not understand the ways of the Lord and were confused about our decision. However, we loved them all and would miss them dearly.

Eventually we gave away all that we had to relatives and friends. Our two sons remained in our house under the care of our relatives. My heart ached in such a way. I could not help but cry. As time for our departure got closer, I looked around remembering how many years it took to build our home and our church. I thought about our neighbors, relatives, friends, and the families we loved so much. I was having mix feelings and being very emotional and the tears would not stop. I wished there was an easier way to do this. My heart ached at the thought of leaving our sons. Nevertheless, we had to stay strong for ourselves and for everyone else. We stayed up the night before our departure saying our final good-byes.

Then on May 25, 1989, we got to the airport with all our friends and love ones. This was a very sad day for us. We could barely contain ourselves. Everyone was in tears. We hugged, kissed, and cried until it was time to board the plane. We could not let go of our two sons. Our children experienced a painful moment in their lives. Brothers and sisters just cried on each other's shoulders. At that last moment I felt such a sharp pain running through my heart. It was the hardest thing I had ever had to do, like everything else, I eventually pulled myself together. The love we had for them was a strong bond.

As we parted with tears streaming down our faces, we walked away from everyone to board the plane. This was good-bye until we meet again. We were on our way to America. The flight was very long and very sad. We had our two daughters with us. It was sad to see them say good-bye to their two brothers. We could only think of them as we travelled the many thousands of miles away from them. All I could think of was their sad faces with the tears rolling down our eyes and theirs. It was a memory I would never be able to forget.

Chapter 8

A YEAR OF CHANGES AND MIRACLES

In everything give thanks: for this is the will of God in Christ Jesus concerning you: 1 Thessalonians 5:18"

We arrived in America to our new life in Portland, Oregon. This would be the place we would eventually call home. We were greeted by the nice family we would be living with. Everything was very strange to us. The climate was very cold. Our first night was not very accommodating. The family was not prepared for the four of us which made us very uncomfortable. The food was very different. We had to make many adjustments. We learn fast how to survive in America. Our sadness was overwhelming and our first experience was not welcoming. We were lonely and missed our sons, family, and friends.

We now are living in a foreign country where everything was so very different from what we were used to. We had to learn about the family we living with. It was not easy to adjust to a new culture in someone else's home. We did try our very best to make things work out. The culture shock was the worst part of all of this. We were grateful to this family for allowing us to stay in their home with them though it was a very difficult couple of weeks. We made a few friends in the church we came to be involved in. However, what had been offered to my husband was now not going to happen. We never knew how they made their decision, but one thing we were sure of; God had brought us here to use the calling and gifts in our lives in this country.

The meeting my husband had with this pastor was disappointing. I looked at him and wondered to myself, how can this be where was the love of God in him? Was God in this man? How could he preach the gospel to the people without the love of God within him? He was a great disappointment to us. I truly began to feel like a Sarah living the life of faith and trust. We were very home sick and missed all the things we were used to having. And now the offer to my husband was no more. we felt hurt and alone.

After a couple weeks we were ask to find a new place to live. We moved to another family's home who had a two-year-old boy. They were happy to have us as their son would have our two girls to play. For the next month we trusted in God to show us what we should do. We continued to attended the church and meet other people. We knew God was in all that was happening to us. We did not give up. Our faith was in

God not in what man could do for us. In our time of need we asked the Lord for His guidance. Even though a man may go back on his word, we knew God never goes back on His word. His word became our source of strength every day. My heart was very grieved by all the disappointments we had already faced; we knew our great God would work out all things for good in our lives.

We remained with this family for another couple weeks. When we found we had to leave, we begin to cry out to the Lord to give us some answers so we knew He was still leading us. In His faithfulness the Lord spoke to us of Abraham and his son Isaac. He reminded us of how Abraham obeyed God and how God honored his faith by providing the sacrificial lamb. He began to show us. He was with us and would take care of us. We were surrounded with His love even if we did not feel love from the people around us. His love was always with us. From that day onwards things were very different for us. We were lonely for fellowship all we could do was rely on the love of God and His peace to carry us through this time in our life. We trusted in God's word everyday to be fruitful in our time of need. He never failed us.

We had needs that only the Lord could provide for us. We kept our eyes and faith on the words of God's promises to supply our needs. We never got too comfortable in other people's homes. We had very little money left as we gave money to every family where we stayed. The money was running out. Never the less we give thanks to the lord as we trusted in him. We were blessed to meet a family whom later introduce us to their friends who were leaving town soon for an extended

A Year of Changes and Miracles

vacation. Eventually we were asked by their friends to house sit in their home for a month while they were gone.

We decided to accept the offer and moved into their home. We continued to miss our sons very much now we were able to make phone calls and talk to them. Our two girls felt free to watch television and sleep in late. We were in a home by ourselves. I was able to cook delicious meals for the first time in America. We enjoyed our time there and thanked God for this family who trusted us and allowed us to live in their home. As the time approached for this family to return, we made a decision to fast and pray trusting God for directions as to what He would have us to do next.

As we were waiting on the Lord for His leading, we had a visit from two ministers from the church. We were not sure why they came to visit us, but the look on their faces told us this was not good. We could tell by the way they greeted us this was not going to be a good visit. Their greeting was cold and they spoke with much arrogance in their voices. What they had to say was not Christ like. There was no compassion and they showed no interest in what our needs were or our calling in the ministry. None of that was of any importance to them whatsoever. Their words to us were this was not the place for us and we should return to Trinidad. There was nothing they could do to help us. My husband interrupted them and told them to stop talking.

He said, "We know when God is speaking and when the devil is talking and right now God is not speaking. The voice and the words we are hearing are not from God."

Then my husband suggested they leave. We could not believe what had just been said to us. In our many years of serving the Lord this was the most despicable thing we had heard from men who called themselves ministers of God.

We knew this is was not from God. This was truly of the devil we never allowed what they said to hold us captive or to doubt our God. We never let the disappointments in man keep us down. We fought every bit of discouragement that came towards us and kept believing our God was able to provide for all our needs. We cast all our cares upon Him for we knew He cared for us. We had depended on the Lord and He had taken care of us ever since we had arrived in this country. This was going to be a very long journey for us, and we were prepared through faith not to give up.

Delight thyself also in the lord: and he shall give thee the desires of thine heart" Psalms 27:4

Our delight was in our lord. Every day we read the scriptures and built our lives on faith. The word of God kept us strong. We had God's promise to never to leave us alone or forsake us. He promised to watch over us, to bless us, and to keep us. We lived each day with hope, faith, and God's amazing grace. We were not about to give way to the devil and his schemes. We came by faith and would live by faith in our Lord. We had served the Lord and trusted in Him for everything so many times before and He had never failed us. We knew He would not fail us now.

Weeks went by and we were invited to a church picnic. While at the picnic we meet a couple who had two girls with the same names as our girls. We had a good time at the picnic and became friends with them. This couple invited us to preach in various meetings and we accepted every offer we got. My husband and I felt we were finally doing what the Lord had called us here to do. Time after time he got the opportunity to preach. We never turned down any offer we received. We eventually left the church where we knew it was time for us to move out and move on to where the Lord could use the gifts and callings in our lives.

Our God Shall Supply All Our Needs+

"My God shall supply all your needs, according to his riches in glory By Christ Jesus. "Philippians 4:19"

It was getting close to the time we'll have to leave the home where we were house-sitting. The owners would be on their way home. We had to find a place to live. We've been looking. And had only one week to find a home. We began to fast and pray for God to grant us a home rent free. We had very little money left. There was not enough to rent a place of our own. Then my husband received an invitation to preach at a men's luncheon meeting. A friend drove us since we did not own a car. When we got there, we were introduced to more people, one of whom God would use to be a blessing to us very soon. After the meeting was over, one of the minister was so impressed by my husband's singing and preaching he invited him to come back to preach for the evening meeting.

We were greeted by many people at the meeting. It was a real blessing to be there. I knew God had something for us, I did not know what it was. I just felt the Holy Spirit so strong around us. We met many business people from many different walks of life. Some offered to help us in whatever we needed. I made mention to a few of them we needed a home to live in by the end of that month as we were house sitting and the family would be back by the end of the next week. Without knowing these people, I told them what our needs were and shared my heart with them how God had brought us to America. These people began to pray and bless us and even gave us an offering. We were tremendously blessed that afternoon.

We went home with praises in our heart to God. Our friend had watched our girls for us and we told them what had happened at the luncheon. They said they had been praying for us that morning for a miracle for us. The evening came and my husband left to preach at the evening meeting. I stay at home with our girls we prayed and believed God would give us a miracle of a home or send us back to Trinidad. We were confident something good would happen.

Later that night a man shows up at the home where we were staying. Telling me God spoke to him about us. He'd" met my husband that morning. He carried two large bags of food and a huge bouquet of beautiful flowers in his hands. He said the flowers were specifically for me. I would not let him in the house since my husband was not there. I called a friend who came over and met with the man for me. They talked and then our friend said it was alright. He stood in the doorway so as not to alarm us in any way. Then he said God had told him to give us a house to live in.

I could hardly believe what I was hearing. I asked him how much the rent would be and he said there will be no rent charged.

"It is free for you guys to live in," he said and then he asked me if I would like to see the house.

I was not sure I wanted to go see the house without my husband, our friend assured me it was okay and agreed to go with us. My two girls, my friend, and I went to see the house. As soon as we walked in I knew this was what I had been feeling at the meeting. The man gave me the keys to the house and offered to help furnish it for us the next day. I looked at him and asked if God had spoken something specific about us to him. He told me he would tell us what the Lord had told him about us the next day. He wanted my husband to see the house first. We left and went back to where we were staying. I thanked the man and then asked our friend to stay with us until my husband got home from the meeting.

As soon as the man left, our friend, my girls, and I started to praise the Lord. We knew this was an answer to our prayers. They could hardly wait until their dad got home from his meeting.

After the meeting was over the people gathered around my husband to pray for him. They prayed for a home for us not knowing God had already answered that pray. They all blessed him as he left for home. He came in the door announcing everyone had prayed God would give us a home to live in. Then he told us on the way home one of the people from the meeting took him to see a house that was vacant and asked if it was suitable for us.

As he was talking and describing the house, our girls shouted out, "Dad, we have got that house. A man came and visited us, He took us to see the house with our friend and we have the keys. God did a miracle!"

When I finally had a chance to tell him what had happened, he looked at me and we both begin to praise the Lord. We were very happy! The next day the man came to visit us as he had promised and took us all over to the house. As we entered the house the man began to tell us the story of how God had given him a vision of a colored family coming into the area and would need a place to live. God told him to clean and paint this vacant house he owned and wait for the family to come. He told us this happened a year ago. That morning when he saw us at the meeting, the Lord told him we are that family for the house. We were surprised and blessed at what he said.

My husband asked him if he could remember the time God spoke to him and the man said was November a year ago. My husband said him it was the same time we made the announcement to the church. We would be leaving the ministry in Trinidad to go to America. The timing was in God's plan for us. The next day he bought the furnishings we needed for the house and blessed us in so many ways. He was truly a blessing from the Lord. We saw the hand of God in our lives so many times. God truly supplied all our needs according to His riches. We moved out of the house where we had been house sitting, telling the family how very grateful we were for their kindness, their trust, and believing in us enough to let us live in their home for that month. We thanked God for them and prayed that the Lord's blessings would be on them always.

We were so happy to be in a place we could call home. We knew God was in control of our lives and everything would work out the way the Lord planned for us. As we were settling down in this new place, we were able to talk to our sons in Trinidad about all that God was doing. They were experiencing their own struggles and loneliness being away from us. Life for them was very hard. They were learning to be strong and hold on to their faith hoping one day we would be united as a family again. They missed us as much as we missed them. We were able to spend time more often on the phone and just to hear their voices brought joy to us. Every day was a day closer to them coming to be with us here in America. We knew somehow it would be soon.

We continued to visit churches and meet more and more people. We started a Bible study in the home where we were living. We invited people to come and they enjoyed listening to my husband teach the Word of God. We had a great time in the presence of the Lord. This was a blessing to everyone that came. Then one day a couple called and asked for counsel as they were having marriage problems. We counseled with them several times and they eventually gave their hearts to God and became believers. We advised them to find a church to worship. Where they felt comfortable. They found a church, and started attending, and decided to be baptized. They wanted us to be present for their baptism as we were responsible for leading them to the Lord. We had a friend who drove us to the church so we could be there to witness this couple's baptism.

We arrive at the church late and there was no seat vacant for us.

As my husband was looking around for seats for us, a tall man walked up to him, introduced himself, and said, "God told me to give you a car."

After he said this to my husband, he turned and walked away. We didn't know what to think. We had never seen this man before and when the service was over, we didn't see him again. As we were leaving, he approached us and offered to drive us to his home to get the car he said he had for us. We then realized this man was serious. He was actually going to give us a car. My husband mentioned we came with friends and the man agreed to wait for us. Our friends agreed to drive us to the man's house to get the car. We followed him to his house, and sure enough he gave us a four-door Chevy in good working condition. We knew this was an answer to our prayers. We had prayed and asked God to provide a car; we didn't know exactly how it would happen, because we had no money to purchase one.

Later we went to visit the guy and express to him how thankful we were to him for being obedient to the Lord, we never saw him again after that night. When we inquired about him, no one knew of him, and we were unsuccessful in locating him. We praised the Lord for providing everything for us. Food, clothes, finances, whatever our need, our heavenly Father provided for us. As we lived by faith in the Lord, things worked out for us every day. I reminded myself of the scriptures I had read about having faith in God. "The just shall live by faith" became the song of my heart. The word of God is life and truth. He has promised life in abundance. I knew nothing else but to trust in the living God and to depend on His grace. Which we did, all our every need was met above and beyond what we even dreamed of asking for.

Above and Beyond What We Can Think or Ask

My husband continued to preach in churches everywhere he got an offer. I was asked many times to share my testimony in the women's meetings. I went wherever I was invited and gave honor and glory to Jesus, the Savior of my life. I would speak about God's amazing grace and power. I counted it a joy and a privilege to share what God had done in my life over the years, and to let people know He would do the same for them if they would only believe.

While we visited one church after another, we met pastors who encouraged us and gave us opportunities to minister in their churches. Some of these ministers did not know much about deliverance ministry. Or had the wrong idea about what it is about. This has become one of the most powerful ministries in our world today. It's the power of God unto salvation for people who need to be delivered. From a lifestyle that held them captive. We met a businessman in one of the meetings. Where my husband was preaching this would prove to be another great blessing from the Lord.

At the end of the meeting he introduced himself to us and invited us to his church on Sunday to meet his pastor. He'd mention to his pastor. My husband had a deliverance ministry. And would be good if they met. He offered to come and drive us so we can visit his church with him on Sunday. We were introduced to the pastor and to the church staff. This was the first time we had ever been introduced to a church staff. We were invited back to this church the next Sunday. The same businessman came and drove us there. My husband was asked to preach a couple more times. I join the church choir and was asked to share my testimony. This was a nice place to be we settled in this church as our home church. The pastor asked what our needs were and he offered to help in any way possible. They offered us a sponsorship that changed our life here in America. And did above and beyond what we had hoped for to bless us. Truly the hand of God worked through this church.

I can honestly say when men obey the Lord things happen for His glory. This is what this pastor did for us. He understood about deliverance ministry. And how the power of God, was evident in our lives and our ministry. Most people do not understand this type of ministry. Some people have a wrong concept about such a ministry. This pastor recognized the calling on our lives and was willing to allow the teaching in his church. He was used by God to fulfill the plan of God in our lives.

Things were very difficult for us when we first came to America. As we were waiting on the Lord, there were times we felt defeated and alone. However, we refused to allow discouragement to dominate or control us. Our faith was not in the words of men. We realized the only power is in God's word. He fought our battles for us. Yes, we have had hard times when we did not feel anything. Working out for us and then the Lord would answer our cry. There is no one like our heavenly Father. He knows the plans He has for us; we just had to remain obedient to His call. God would always fight for us every step of the way. We are most grateful to this pastor and his church for everything they did on our behalf. We thank God for the people who richly blessed us while we were there.

Sometime later we were ministering in a meeting. When I shared, about our sons in Trinidad, and how much we missed them. We believe God for a miracle so I could travel back to Trinidad, and help them get their immigration papers ready. The Spirit of God witnessed to someone that night they should do something to bless us. The next morning the phone rang and a woman. I had never met said to me God spoke to her she should be a blessing, and she would like to purchase the plane tickets for our boys to come to America. She then told me to call her when I was ready to leave for Trinidad.

We prayed and within a few weeks our sons' papers were ready. Either my husband or I would to go to Trinidad to be with them when they went before the American consulate I called this woman and let her know. One of us needed to leave and she brought the tickets for our sons. As she said she would. She was very happy to do this. She said while I was speaking in the meetings, the Holy Spirit had told her she should do this for us. She wanted to be sure the Lord was speaking to her and when she got home the Lord spoke to her again to do this. So in obedience to the Lord she blessed our family.

As the time for the trip to Trinidad to bring our sons to America approached, I travelled with my husband to a church he had preached in before. My husband and this pastor had become good friends. He would have my husband preach for him very often. This particular Sunday the pastor told my husband that God had spoken to him. And told him to buy the plane ticket we needed. He didn't know we needed to go to Trinidad to bring our sons to America. We had not told him anything about this pending trip. We knew this had to be the Lord. That Sunday the people blessed us with a plane ticket to Trinidad and an elderly gentleman gave us a big check for spending money. I knew the Lord would provide for this trip.

I had been fasting and praying and the Holy Spirit spoke to me and said. I would be going home for our boys. Originally we thought my husband would be the one to go. Instead the Lord spoke to me I'd be the one to go. Soon the day came for me to leave, my husband and my daughters told me how much they loved me and they would miss me. I had never left my girls before and I'd never travelled by myself before either. This was very scary for me. I prayed all during the flight. I didn't know at the time. This was the beginning of many trips to come.

I kept praising God for all He had done for us in the one year we had been in America. We had lived by faith and experienced miracle after miracle. Going home was another miracle. This had been an overwhelming journey for me. I'd been at many cross roads and gone through many twists and turns along the way, but through it all I never gave up. I always trusted in Jesus for my answers. I could never turn my back on the Lord. He's everything to me in every way. The struggles I encountered in my life only made me stronger and more determined to follow Jesus. This is my desire to always do what He called me to do. My God is a great God!

I arrived in Trinidad and was greeted by our sons and relatives and friends. This was a happy and a sad time. They were all happy I was home. Even though, I would have to leave again this only time. I'll be taking our sons with me. I was very excited to see everyone after a year. It felt good to be home, to relax and eat the delicious food we missed so much in America. I was so happy just being home and I loved seeing everyone.

The day arrived when we had to go to the immigration department to get the legal papers for our sons to leave Trinidad it was a day of trials. A lot of things happened as we went through the process, we finally got their papers. I was happy when it was all over now they have their papers in order. They were overjoyed! They had not been with us for over a year. Soon we'll be united. With all the stuff that took place in Trinidad and all the unrest, God kept us safe while we were there and we were able to leave within a few days. This was another very sad day for our other family. Friends and relatives. We went through the tears and good-bye hugs again. This is never easy for anyone to have to say good-bye to loved ones.

As we were leaving, I said to them, "This will never end. Every time I come home we will do this over and over again."

We boarded the plane, and watched their sad faces from the windows as we took off. We were on our way to America. I carried the love for the people I had nurtured in the Lord and all my family and relatives in my heart. All I could do for them was to continue to pray for them. Leaving loved ones behind not knowing when I would see them again was a very emotional time for me. However, I knew I had to move on with my life. After the long flight, we arrived in America and were greeted with so much love from my husband and our two daughters and friends. What a joy to see our sons and daughters hug each other through tears of joy. The boys hugged their dad; full of love so emotional. This was a very wonderful time of reunion for us. We were together at last and nothing would separate us again.

We were extremely happy God had brought us together. We had waited a long time for this moment. We praised God for making things happen for us. By faith all things work together for good. All the waiting and trusting in the Lord brought us the victory in Christ. We arrived home to our little miracle house happy just to be a united family. Our sons had to learn to adjust to the culture, the climate, and the food. This would be a very big change for them. We knew life in America would be full of challenges for them. The school systems were probably the biggest cultural shock. They learned fast. Another phase of our life was about to begin, but for right now we just rejoiced in having our family altogether in one place!

Chapter 9

BLESSED ARE THEY THAT MOURN FOR THEY SHALL BE COMFORTED

We continued in the ministry stronger and more powerful than we've been, soon we were to face some battles in the church we were attending. They did not need us anymore so we left and moved on. We went wherever the Lord would lead us. Where we were accepted, we stayed. Wherever God opened doors for us, my husband would minister. We lived in the same house for a few years, and then we were asked to move out by the brother of the guy who gave us the house. He wanted the house for his son. We eventually moved to a bigger house that was provided for us by the businessman who had invited us to his church and introduced us to his pastor. This man remained a constant blessing to us.

My husband and I lived through unfortunate contacts with many untrustworthy, arrogant people who made promises; they did not keep until we realized we could no longer depend on man for anything. Only God's word is truth and our faith had to be only in God. We had to keep our eyes on the Lord, continue to live by faith, and expect miracles as part of our daily lives.

More Tests and Trials

One year after I came home from Trinidad with our sons, we discovered our youngest daughter had a cyst on her spleen. We had no health insurance. We did not know anything about insurance or where to take her for the care she desperately needed. We were afraid we might lose her. A friend of ours told us of a hospital we could take her to have her examined by a pediatrician. We didn't know what to do or what to expect. We took our friend's advice. And with help from another friend brought us. Since we didn't know where the hospital was located and stayed the entire day with us as the Doctors examined our daughter.

I was beginning to get very concerned at all these doctors coming in to check on our little girl. After a couple hours they wanted to talk with me. I was afraid of hearing what the doctors had to say. They told me she had to have emergency surgery. to remove the cyst from her spleen or she could die. I was in shock! How could this happen to our little girl? I broke down and began to cry. I tried to explain to the doctors we did not have any money or health insurance. They looked at me and said saving the child's life was more important to them. Someone else came in to talk with me about all the arrangements. And schedules, for the surgery. I was warned I had to make the decision the same day. I agreed to the surgery without my husband's consent, and signed the paper work for

Blessed Are They that Mourn for They Shall be Comforted

her surgery. I believed this was a life and death situation for our daughter. The nurses were very assuring and encouraged me saying our daughter would be in good hands.

I looked at our friend and said, "This is my karma, I'm living my name?"

He assured me everything would be alright; the doctors knew what to do to save her life. I thought about how my parents must have felt many years ago. when they had to make decisions like this for my life. Fear gripped me all I could think about was how young she was! She had to live! Nothing can go wrong!

God, where are you? I thought to myself. *Why this? Why now?* I was strong and yet I was weak. I could hardly think straight. Then I looked at our friend and he was crying, He felt the pain I was experiencing. He was a very good friend to our family and always there when we needed him. He took me home and I broke the sad news to my husband and the other three kids. Everyone started to cry. All this happened on our wedding anniversary! It was a day I will never forget. We prayed that night for our little girl's life. We asked God to heal her and give her back to us as a healthy little girl.

We were attending a church where everyone knew us. We were truly loved by so many of the people. We received so much support from them. My husband also had a pastor friend who stood with us throughout this difficult time. We knew God was in control of all that happened in our life, yet I was feeling this was too much for us as a mother. I did not want anything to go wrong for my little girl. My faith started to waver, and I started to lose confidence in my belief.

My husband had to be strong for me and he encouraged me. He reminded me of all God's promises to heal. He reminded me. We had been living by faith all our lives, and told me this was only a trial for our family. This was hard for me to not to think about what would happen if something went wrong. It's easy to listen to the devil when we are under pressure. I knew my husband was right and I had to put my trust in God who had been there for us time and time again.

The journey to the hospital was a very sad one on the day of the surgery. When we got to her room, we gathered around our little girl and my husband anointed her with anointing oil. We prayed over her for a successful surgery and a quick recovery. I was very nervous about the whole thing. I started to cry. My emotions got the better of me. I just could not help myself. The surgery took four and a half hours. I have always been a tower of strength in our family, but this time I was weak. I was an emotional mess as we waited to hear the results. The surgery went very well. The doctors were very pleased. Our daughter was amazing! I was allowed to stay with her the eight days she was in the hospital. She made a marvelous recovery. God was faithful to us and answered our prayers!

We received so much support from the church family and all our friends. It was amazing to feel the love of our Christian family during such a difficult time. Even though I was feeling down, I never let the devil have control. I knew I could trust in God. Even in my weakness His strength was made perfect. He made me strong though at the time I felt I was falling under the load. I refused to let that load of heaviness wear me down. After our daughter was discharged from the hospital, we went home a happy family. We praised the Lord for His love, mercy, and goodness towards us.

During the weeks ahead we witnessed our daughter regain her health. She was completely healed by the Lord's hands. We had to continue doctor's visits for follow up appointments to be sure she was doing well. They were amazed at how well she recovered from her surgery. Her siblings were very happy to have her home. They knew God had taken care of their sister throughout the whole hospital experience. Once again our faith was being tested. Our children were in constant prayer for their sister in the hospital. She grew up to be a very strong, healthy, beautiful young girl. She always remembered to thank Jesus for her life knowing. He's with her was very special to her as she grew up.

God had done so much for us in so many ways. He never let us down. We were always confident of His hands on our lives. We knew He would supply our every need. Every struggle we encountered we called upon the Lord to sustain us. In His faithfulness, no matter what kind of trial we faced. Though we missed our loved ones in Trinidad especially during these trials, we stood strong together and relied on each. We had no other choice.

More Major Changes in Our Lives

A few months after our daughter's surgery we suddenly faced a severe financial battle. We were attending a church where my husband was the administrator. The pay was very little for a family of six, and we found we had to do something to help bring in more income. I enrolled in a nursing program that would qualify me to work and earn a salary. This was a hard for me to do. I had always been a stay at home mom. This would be a major change in our lives. I was soon employed at a nursing facility full time. All this was hard for me since I had never worked outside the home. My dedication had always been solely focused on my husband, children, and the ministry. Our lives were changing in a big way.

I knew God was leading me because of the favor. I received from people I met. The Lord had placed them in my life to help me. This was very hard for my husband and my children to see me going to work every day. I told them to just bless me and let me go in God's grace. I promised them I would always. Be the wife and mother God had made me to be, and I have kept that promise until this very day. When I would come home tired at the end day, my family were the ones that made my day a joyful one. I would always have dinner ready on time. We would sit down and enjoy a delicious meal together every day. My life was always about making them happy. They always came first no matter what the cost. I maintained a good home and family lifestyle even though I was now working a full time job outside the home.

We had a very happy home. There was always joy and laughter along with strong discipline. I took time for my family. Together my husband and I taught our children the values of having a loving and respectable life. We taught them to be loyal and trustworthy so as they grew up to be adults they would be able to face their struggles with an inner strength. Our children were quick to learn and quick to break every rule they were taught, however, they were always loved. I gave them my all.

We never missed a church service. We were always on time. Our children watched us go through many tough times and struggles, in the ministry they saw us continue to live by faith. It was not easy to tell your children to trust in God for everything when they had needs of their own and needed an immediate answer. They were always looking for results to prayer and many times their prayers were answered by a miracle. That is how they learned to experience faith in God in their own way.

When we were asked how we handled our problems in a foreign country, we always told people we lived by faith and trusted in God. Many times people looked astonished and could not understand how we could live this way. Some people turn to different methods for answers, we had learned to turn to our God. This was the only answer we had to give.

When my children needed answers or were facing trials at school, we did our best to assure them of God's love and grace. Sometimes I felt it was not enough for them especially when they were teenagers. Their friends often had different values and they faced a lot of peer pressure. We knew this was an ongoing battle for them.

As things were beginning to be stirred up at the church where my husband was involved in ministry, we felt it was time for us to move on. We felt our children needed to be with Christian people more their age group. We found a church that our kids loved where there were lots of young people their age. It had a very vibrant youth ministry. The youth pastor and his wife loved them and took our kids under their wings. They loved and blessed them and our kids got involved in the youth and the dance ministry. They began to grow in their faith and loved being in the presence of other young people who could the word of God.

This was a very exciting time in their lives, and our family become very involved in this church. My husband became a cell group leader and we hosted one of the cell groups in our home. The group grew and the people were eager to know more about the Lord. I joined the prayer ministry and the choir. I still enjoyed singing for the Lord. Our family was very happy to be in this church. Everyone was so friendly and the love of God was felt by everyone. The love of God was real to our children. Their zeal and motivation for the Lord was amazing! We felt like family to all the families we met, and our children developed a real bound with the young people there. There were many opportunities for our children to get involved in the ministry and to continue to grow. This was a blessing for our children!

We had only been in this church for about a year and a half when we had to leave. My husband accepted an offer to move to California to work in a church there. We had mixed feeling about moving out of Oregon. My husband made all the arrangements for us to move and we had to say good-bye to all our friends. It was very hard for our kids to leave the church where they had developed such wonderful relationships. I had to resign my job; I had grown close to a few of my co-workers and my supervisor. She wished me well and said if I ever moved back to Oregon she would hire me back. Almost everyone spoke about us coming back some day even though we had not even moved yet.

We moved to a small town name Lodi in northern California. It was a very nice place to live and raise a family. The church was very large. We were amazed! These were the richest people we had ever been around. Even though we were welcomed by the pastor and congregation, we did not feel at home there. We felt as if we were just there making up numbers. There was no ministry for my husband, my children tried very hard to fit in with the youth, it soon began to look like this was not the place for us.

We did make a couple of friends while we were there. When our oldest daughter was about to turn sixteen, I told my friend what I wanted to do. This friend took it upon herself to plan a big surprise party for our daughter. It was a very special time for her. We all had a marvelous time. This friend was a real blessing to our family and we were thankful to God for her.

However, we continued to feel we were not supposed to be there and decided to move back to Oregon. We asked a very good friend there to help us find a home to live in when we returned which he did. We reunited with all our friends. We were happy to see them as much as they were happy to see us. We started our life right back up in the church where we had left. I went back to my old job. My former boss was very happy to have me back. It did not take long for us to get settled back in to life in Oregon.

My husband started to work with one of his friends in the construction business and also preached the gospel wherever he was invited. Every day with the Lord was a good day, even if things were not going good for us. We eventually got back into ministry in the previous church and our life was rich with the fullness of God's blessings. The love of the Lord continued to shine in our lives. One day I said to our family. I did not think we would ever move again. We had learned the hard way not to trust the words and promises of man. Our children were happy to see all their friends again and liked the idea of not having to move again.

Our oldest son began working in construction with my husband and his friend. Our second son and our two daughters were back in school and loving it. It was a joy for all of us to be back in Oregon. We all found our own place in ministry. My children were very much involved in the youth dance ministry.

Tragedy Strikes Our Family

We had only been back in Oregon one year when tragedy struck our family. This was the worst thing that had ever happened to us. On April 11th after a long day at work, my husband picked the kids up from school and then picked me up from work. I was cooking dinner when our oldest son came home from his job.

He was very happy and jokingly said to me, "Mom, I have a meeting to attend. Can you come with me?"

I said that I could not and he joked around with us as he changed and prepared to leave. He said he had to go as he did not want to get caught in the traffic. He walked out to his car, looked at me and smiled.

Then he came back into the house and said, "Mom, I have something to tell you. I will tell you when I get home tonight."

Blessed Are They that Mourn for They Shall be Comforted

I insisted for him to tell me before he left but he said, "Later." Then he walked to his black BMW and drove away to his meeting. We stood by the window and watched as he drove away waving and smiling. For some unknown reason, I watched the car drive down the street until I could not see him anymore. I wished he had told me what he wanted to say before he left. Little did I know that it would be the last time I would see my son smile.

April 12th started like every other morning. I looked out the window for our son's car. It was not there. He had not come home the night before. We assumed he must have stayed at his friend's house. My husband took me to work that morning as our son did not come home to take me. I left home wondering why he had not called us to let us know he was not coming home. Our second son and I would normally stay up until he came home, but I was extremely tired and told our second son to stay awake and wait for his brother. I went to sleep, but I did not sleep well. I had very unusual feelings. I could not understand why I felt the way I did.

My husband was ill and I thought that was why I could not sleep. I prayed for my husband to feel better. I still had a weird feeling the next morning, but I paid no attention to how I felt. I had to work and the kids had to get to school. We tried calling our son, but there was no answer. We assumed he was still asleep at his friend's house.

As I was on my way up the elevator to the floor where I worked, I began to pray for strength from the Lord. My scripture that morning was Psalm 25, "To you O Lord I lift up soul. O God I trust in you." I trusted my feelings into the Lord's hands. Whatever I was feeling the Lord would take care of me. My husband went back home to pick up the kids to take them to school. When he arrived at the house he saw the county coroner's car parked at the house. A strange man was walking away from the house toward the car.

As my husband approached this man, he said to my husband, "Your son was a fatally in a road accident."

Not knowing what the guy meant, my husband asked the man what hospital our son was in. The guy then told my husband that our son had died in the accident. Before my husband could say another word, the guy left him standing there. My husband could hear our three other children screaming inside the house. This cold uncaring man from the coroner's office had told our kids this horrible news without an adult being there with them. He just told them the bad news and left. He never offered a kind word to them or offered to call an adult to be with them. What a cruel thing to have done to our children.

I had gotten to work at seven and at eight forty-five I was paged to come to the office. When I got there I saw our three children sitting there. Their eyes were red. I could tell something had happened. They just stared at me as if they could not speak. I approached them and asked what was going on.

My oldest daughter told me that their daddy had something to tell me. I walked into the room where my husband was and looked into his eyes. I knew it was not good. He looked at me as if he did not know what to say.

I then asked, "Whose mother, yours or mine?" assuming someone had passed away.

"We need to be strong for the children," he said and then told me we had lost our son in a car accident.

When I asked him when it had happened, he said the night before at around eleven o clock. I tried to ask whose car he was in and who was driving, but suddenly all I could think of was I was never going to see my son again or hear his voice. I felt numb like a part of me had died. I broke down and asked God why He had taken our son from me? How was I going to live? What about his brother and sisters? What about his is dad? How were we ever going to handle our boy being gone out of our lives? Why us? Why our family? I could no longer think about anything. I just walked towards an open window and looked out at the blue sky with tears in my eyes. I watched the white clouds passing by as if to say good-bye to me.

This was the worst day of our lives. My husband and the children took me into the chapel next to the office. We all were crying. It was a day we would never forget as long as we lived. All I wanted to do was to see my son. We were soon surrounded by the Chaplin and all my co-workers. They were so compassionate to us.

After a couple of hours we got a call from the church telling my husband to bring us to the church. The pastors and their wives were waiting for us with open arms of love and comfort.

Our grief and sadness spread to those that came to be with us on this sad day. My husband then had to make phone calls to our relatives in Trinidad to tell them the bad news. How I wished they could be with us. My heart was bleeding for the loss of our son. I felt as if it was a bad dream. We remained at the church for almost the full day.

Later as I walked into the house, I could hear my son's voice in the distance. I felt helpless as I watched my three kids grieving the loss of their brother. I could not find the right words to say to them nor could my husband. We did not know what to say to each other. We were hurting very deep in our hearts. Later in the evening the phone started ringing as our relatives called us from Trinidad and Canada to give their love and support. It was not easy when everyone was crying so hard.

The loss of a child is the worst thing any parent can experience. There is no way to explain the unbearable pain in your heart. It stays there and never goes away. That night as friends were gathering at the house to come be with us, we could not stop crying. We knew in our hearts our son went to heaven, but we could not sleep. We stayed up late though we were tired from sorrow and pain. When we did finally get a little sleep, we awoke the next morning feeling even worse. We hugged each other and cried. None of us could understand why he had to leave us, but there were no answers.

He died on April 11th. His birthday was April 15th. We did not get to view his body until the fifteenth. We all walked into the funeral home where he was kept. We walked up to him. I remember leaning over him causing my face to touch him. We all stood there and looked at him with tears rolling down our faces. We touched him and talked to him. Somehow in the midst of this God gave us His peace.

We had not been allowed to see his body before that day. We were treated horribly by the coroner's office attendants. All the information they had on our dead son was wrong. The news media had everything wrong. We did not give them permission to release anything. They just did what they wanted to do. All we were told was there was an investigation going on. They said it is a vehicular homicide and the police could not answer our any of our questions about the accident.

We had a funeral to plan so we did not push for details at the time. We put our love for our son and brother into beautiful words to say good-bye and to remember him by. We wanted to express who he was and his love to us. His charming smile would never be forgotten. We thought about how happy he was when he bought his first car, a BMW! The joy of life bubbled out of him. Now he was gone and we had all these memories to cherish. However, the days before the funeral were long and cold, filled with sadness.

Our Celebration of Our Son's Life

The funeral was on Monday, April 17th. It was a day we had to say our final good-byes. We all felt a deep pain inside our hearts. We arrived at the church where we were greeted by members and friends. This day demanded all my strength. I wanted to be strong for my kids. I wanted everything to be just right for our good-bye to our beloved son. We had decided to make it more like a birthday celebration than a funeral. Even with all the sadness and the tears, there was a little joy in the service. He loved humor and there was a lot of humor. He touched as many or more lives in his death than when he was alive.

Everyone who wanted to speak had their chance. My husband and I asked a friend to read our good-bye for us. We could not have done it. His brother and two sisters read their most precious thoughts, shared their love for him, and express all that he meant to them in their lives growing up. I was crying, but I had control over my feelings. His favorite scriptures were read and his favorite hymns were sung. This was a moment just for him. In our time of sadness the Lord made us strong. He gave us an inner strength and a peace in our hearts knowing we would see our son again in heaven.

It was a rainy day, very cold and depressing when we entered the church, but after the service the sun came out and brighten as we proceeded to the cemetery to lay his body to rest. I don't know where I got the strength as the reality hit me that this is not a dream, it was real. I keep asking myself how I was going to be able to live without my son. As these words filled my mind, the pain got deeper in my heart. Then I looked at my husband and three kids and wondered what they were thinking. How were we as a family to get over this loss? As our teary eyes met, it was like we were saying to each other, we know your pain. It's like part of us was gone. We comforted each other knowing somehow God would heal the wounds. The presence of God was felt very richly amongst us that day.

When we arrived home after we left the cemetery, the house felt cold and empty. Our son and brother were missing. We knew then our life would never be the same. We just had to turn everything we were feeling over to the Lord and depend on His love and grace to bring us through this horrible tragedy. All I could only think of was the baby I had given birth to twenty-one years ago was gone. There was a sting in my heart that I still feel even today. We purposed in our lives to always keep his memory alive though at first it was hard to think of someone so precious to us had become a memory. The memory became our treasure, one that would last forever.

Though I fought against it, I went into a depression and had to be medicated. God delivered me from the ups and downs of depression and I am thankful for my devoted and praying husband and children who read the scriptures over me even when I could not respond to them. The power of the word of God gave them His strength and gave me solace. One year after our son's passing we were fortunate to be able to travel back to Trinidad, his birth place, and hold a very nice memorial service with family and friends in his memory. None of our relatives had been able to come to America to say their good-byes.

My mom returned to America with us. I thought she was going to live with us but she did not like living here. Nine months later I had to take her home to Trinidad. I was happy to see my siblings, their families, and our friends again, but it was hard to say good-bye again. I would do this many times in the future. When I returned home to America, my oldest daughter was ill and had to have surgery. Thanks be to God we had the support of a church family that was caring enough to stand and pray with us all through these battles. The Lord carried us through as we stood together on God's promise that we are healed by the stripes of Jesus. She had the surgery and made an amazing recovery.

As I prayed for my daughter's healing, I was reminded of what my parents had gone through in their struggles to seek healing for me. I knew where to turn when bad things happened. I called on the name of my Lord, our deliver and healer. He knew all the heartache I had experienced. He dried the tears from my eyes, took all my burdens, and made me who I am today. His word is my truth!

Two years later, we discovered our second son had never really gotten over his brother's death. He carried within him a guilt we did not know about from the night his brother died. Apparently our second son had met his brother earlier that evening while he was playing basketball. His brother had asked him to come with him to play pool, but he wanted to finish his game of basketball and told him he will see him later at the house. That never happened and we never realized these feelings of guilt he had been carrying around as he never opened up to anyone about it. Once we found out, we did all we could to get him help. We did not know the extent of his pain at the loss of his only brother. We prayed he would let God take it from him so he could live with the memories. Our daughters had to deal with their feelings of loss as well. Our family's strength was my husband and his strong faith in God.

The word of God says blessed are they that mourn for they shall be comforted and they that call upon the Lord shall be renewed in their strength (see Matthew 5:4). We are a living testimony of how God rescues His children even in the midst of their grief.

CONCLUSION

All Things Work Together for Good to Those Who Love God

My husband and I have been married over forty-one years at the writing of this book. We now live a quiet and peaceful life as we continue to serve the Lord. Our two daughters are married with children of their own and are currently serving the Lord alongside their husbands.

Our youngest son now resides in Trinidad. We have seven grandchildren and they are our pride and joy. We have continued to travel to Trinidad every three years to visit relatives and friends. We continue to preach the gospel and attend a church where we are comfortable and loved. Our God is so very real to us and has done great things in our lives. He has brought us through the tough times in our life, and has met all our needs time and time again. Every day is a new day with new blessings from the Lord. We continue to give Him all the praise and honor and glory and will continue to do so as long as we live.

Though the journey of my life included struggles, death, victory, sadness, depression, disappointment, and even discouragement over the years, I have trusted in God and kept my faith alive through His word. I have learned to overcome and continue to be more than a conqueror in Him. In all these things I know without the shadow of a doubt that nothing will separate me from the love of my God which is in Jess Christ our Lord.

"And we know that all things work together for good to them that love God, to them who are the called according to his purpose". (Roman 8:28)

Conclusion

ABOUT THE AUTHOR

Karma is currently attending "Life Christian Center" where she is active in the prayer ministry and sings in the Church Choir, she and her husband are both serving on the Pastoral-Care Team. She is passionate to minister to individuals who face life's struggles, and encourages them in the Lord. Her husband Kenneth is a minister who is currently a freelance minister and singer. Karma and her husband travel together to minister the Gospel of God's Saving Power and His Healing Grace.

smmykayra@hotmail.com
sammyk672@gmail.com
www.lifechristiancenter.com

CPSIA information can be obtained at www.ICGtesting.com
Printed in the USA
BVOW11s0747171014

371137BV00014B/398/P